THE TIMOTHY INITIATIVE

New Testament Pastoral Epistles

Greg Kappas and Jared Nelms, EDS.

New Testament Pastoral Epistles
Book Seven in TTI's Foundational Curriculum

© 2012 by The Timothy Initiative

International Standard Book Number: 978-1477582862

All rights reserved. Published and Printed in the United States of America.

Library of Congress Cataloging-in-Publication Data

No part of this book covered by the copyrights heron may be reproduced or copied
in any form or by any means without written permission of the publisher.

Scripture quotations are from: The New King James Version
Copyright © 1979, 1980, 1982 by Thomas Nelson, Inc.
Used by permission. All rights reserved.

First Edition-North America
Second Edition

THE TIMOTHY INITIATIVE

"What you have heard from me in the presence of many witnesses entrust to faithful men who will be able to teach others also."

2 Timothy 2:2

Acknowledgements

TTI gives special gratitude to the Docent Group and the leadership of Glenn Lucke and Jared Wilson (Docent Executive Editor for this project). We thank the Docent writer, Christopher Wiles and Grace Fellowship Staff member, Pastor Larry Starkey who both spent many long hours on this project. Special thanks to Ken & Jackie Kendall who provided an excellent section on Marriage and Family (Appendix). We also are grateful for Dr. Greg Kappas and Rev. Jared Nelms for their extensive additions and revisions to this manuscript.

TTI also gives thanks to Dr. David Nelms, our Founder/President for his vision and influence to see this New Curriculum written. Dr. Nelms has lived humbly to see you succeed greatly in Jesus Christ.

We express our gratitude for the fine, long editorial labor to TTI Executive Editor and Director, Dr. Greg Kappas and the Executive Editorial Assistant and International Director, Rev. Jared Nelms. In addition we thank the entire TTI editorial team of Dr. David Nelms, Rev. Jesse Nelms, Rev. Larry Starkey, Rev. Lou Mancari and Dr. David Nichols. Each of you has given such remarkable grace to us and now to these church planters.

TTI is greatly appreciative of the Grace Fellowship elders, pastors, administrative staff, leaders and GF family. TTI was birthed out of this "church for all nations." Thank you for your generosity in launching this exponential network of church planting movements.

TTI's Board of Directors has given us freedom and focus to excel still more. We are deeply moved by these men and women of God. Our TTI investor base of financial and prayer partners extend around the globe. These individuals, churches, ministries, networks, corporations and organizations are essential and strategic to our collective health and Kingdom impact. Thank you!

We thank the TTI Continental Directors, Regional Directors, National Directors and District/Training Center Leaders for your ministry of love and commitment. You are the ones that forge into new and current frontiers with the Gospel. You truly are our heroes.

Finally, we are forever grateful to you, the church planter. You are planting an orchard, a church-planting center through your local church that will touch your region and the world with the Gospel of Jesus Christ. We are honored to serve the Lord Jesus Christ and you. You will make a difference for our great God as you multiply healthy churches for His glory. We love you and believe in you!

The Timothy Initiative Staff Team
December 2010

This workbook is the seventh of 10 workbooks which assist in equipping church planting leaders to start churches that saturate a region and help reach every man, woman and child with the Good News of our Lord. Below is the list of this initial curriculum.

TTI Curriculum

Workbook Number/Course:

1. Hermeneutics

2. Homiletics

3. Church Planting (New Testament – Acts, Evangelism, Discipleship, Spiritual Life, T4T)

4. Old Testament 1

5. Old Testament 2

6. New Testament Gospels

7. New Testament Pastoral Epistles

8. New Testament General Letters

9. Major Bible Doctrines

10. Apologetics - Church History - Spiritual Warfare

Table of Contents

Introduction: Introduction to the Pastoral Epistles 10

Section 1: 1 Timothy

Chapter 1: Book Outlines & 1 Timothy 1:1-11 14
Chapter 2: 1 Timothy 1:12-20 24
Chapter 3: 1 Timothy 2:1-8 28
Chapter 4: 1 Timothy 2:9-15 30
Chapter 5: 1 Timothy 3:1-7 34
Chapter 6: 1 Timothy 3:8-13 38
Chapter 7: 1 Timothy 5:1-2 42
Chapter 8: 1 Timothy 5:17-20 44
Chapter 9: 1 Timothy 6:6-16 48
Chapter 10: 1 Timothy 6:17-19 52

Section 2: 2 Timothy

Chapter 11: Book Outlines & 2 Timothy 1 58
Chapter 12: 2 Timothy 2 70
Chapter 13: 2 Timothy 3 80
Chapter 14: 2 Timothy 4 86

Section 3: Titus

Chapter 15: Titus 1 94
Chapter 16: Titus 2 102
Chapter 17: Titus 3 106

Section 4: Preaching & Leadership

Chapter 18: Suggestions for Preaching 112

Chapter 19: Godly Leaders 118

Additional Resources

Appendix: Marriage & Family 126

Endnotes 132

Introduction to the Pastoral Epistles

Background: *1 & 2 Timothy* and *Titus* are called the "pastoral letters." The pastoral letters were written from Paul to two pastors in the early church.

The Bible lists *1* and *2 Timothy* together, with *Titus* after. But the order they were written in was:

1 Timothy → *Titus* → *2 Timothy*

Titles: The titles of the books come from the names of the men the letters were written to (Timothy and Titus).

Author: Paul claimed to have written all three letters. He mentions this in the beginning of each letter (*1 Timothy 1:1; 2 Timothy 1:1* and *Titus 1:1*).

In the letters, Paul mentions events in his life (*1 Timothy 1:12-13; 2 Timothy 3:10-11; 4:10, 11, 19, 20*), which would only make sense if he was the author of the letter.

The early church believed that Paul was the author. But recently there has been some debate about who wrote *2 Timothy*.

Audience:

Timothy:
Just like Paul, Timothy was a missionary. Timothy was from a city called Lystra (*Acts 16:1-3*), but was probably converted to Christianity when Paul came to visit (*Acts 14:6, 19*). Timothy was later chosen to come with Paul on his second missionary journey. When Paul was released from prison, Timothy was put in charge of the church in the city of Ephesus.

Timothy was serving in the city of Ephesus and had the responsibility to guide the plans of the church in Ephesus.

Titus:
Titus was born in the city of Antioch (*Galatians 2:1-3*). He met Paul early in his ministry and was converted around 49 AD. Titus accompanied Paul on his third missionary journey.

After Paul was released from prison, the two went to the island of Crete, where Titus was given the task of setting up a church there.

We know from history that Titus did not stay in Crete but rejoined Paul for a brief period. He later returned to Crete, where he remained until the end of his life.

Historical Setting and Purpose:

1 Timothy:
This letter was written between 63-66 AD. Timothy needed to be instructed about how a church should be led. Paul wrote the letter to "defend sound doctrine and maintain sound discipline."[1]

Titus:
This letter was written between 62 and 66 AD. Titus faced many problems in the church in Crete. Paul sent this letter to him to encourage him to be a good church leader.

2 Timothy:
This letter was written between 67-68 AD. This was the last book of the Bible Paul ever wrote before he was executed. Paul was in prison at the time he wrote this letter.

In 64 AD Rome had burned. The Emperor Nero blamed the Christians, and now they were being persecuted. Some Christians were trying to avoid conflict. Paul wrote to Timothy to encourage him to persevere in sharing the Gospel.

Ephesus:
The city of Ephesus was known for false worship. They had built a huge temple to the false goddess Diana. The people there were very wealthy, but they practiced immorality and listened to false teachers. The city had great influence and respect from many other cities. The Gospel called people to stop worshipping false idols, which was not a well-liked message because it hurt the businesses that operated in the city.

Crete:
Crete was an island known for being full of (in Paul's words) "liars, evil beasts [and] lazy gluttons" (*Titus 1:2*). They once had their own government until Rome conquered them in 67 BC, and afterward they resisted the Roman government. The church in Crete had probably been built by Christians who were saved at Pentecost (*Acts 2:11*). There were now many teachers in the church, but they emphasized works of the law and practiced immorality. Therefore, they were false teachers.

Themes:

1 Timothy:
The role of a church leader is to defend sound doctrine and promote solid discipline.

Titus:
Sound doctrine leads to good works.

2 Timothy:
Christians must remain faithful to sound doctrine when being persecuted.[2]

THE TIMOTHY INITIATIVE

SECTION 1: 1 TIMOTHY

Chapter One
Book Outlines and 1 Timothy 1:1-11

Book Overview:

Chapter 1
Sound Doctrine .... Balance

Chapter 2
Proper worship .... Exalting YHWH

Chapter 3
Solid Leadership .... Integrity

Chapter 4
Maintaining Godliness in the assembly .... Excellence

Chapter 5 (1 Timothy 5:1-20; 1 Timothy 6:1, 2)
Maintaining healthy relationships .... Meeting Needs

Chapter 6 (1 Timothy 6:3-21; 1 Timothy 5:21-25)
Pursuing Godliness .... Purity

General Outline of 1 Timothy:

Theme: the policy and practice of the New Testament Church

1. Paul's charge to the assembly of God (*Chapters 1-3*)

    A. The doctrine of the church (*Chapter 1*)
      - His warning of false doctrine (*1 Timothy 1:1-11*)
      - His thanks to God for his ministry (*1 Timothy 1:12-17*)
      - His charge to Timothy concerning his gifts (*1 Timothy 1:18-20*)

    B. The worship in the church (*Chapter 2*)
      - The place of prayer in worship (*1 Timothy 2:1-8*)
      - The place of women in worship (*1 Timothy 2:9-15*)

    C. The leaders of the church (*Chapter 3*)
      - Qualifications for elders (*1 Timothy 3:1-7*)
      - Qualifications for deacons (*1 Timothy 3:8-13*)
      - Qualifications for female deacons (*1 Timothy 3:11*)
      - Obligations to promote godliness (*1 Timothy 3:14-16*)

2. Paul's Charge to the Servant of God (*Chapters 4-6*)

   A. Maintaining godliness in the assembly (*Chapter 4*)
      - Exposing false doctrine (*1 Timothy 4:1-7*)
      - Practice godliness (*1 Timothy 4:8-11*)
      - True doctrine (*1 Timothy 4:12-16*)

   B. Maintaining good relationships with all classes (*Chapters 5-6*)
      - Treatment of the elderly and younger (*1 Timothy 5:1-2*)
      - Treatment of widows who serve (*1 Timothy 5:3-16*)
      - Treatment of ministering elders (*1 Timothy 5:17-25*)
      - Instruction concerning servanthood (*1 Timothy 6:1-6*)
      - Instruction concerning wealth (*1 Timothy 6:6-21*)

Specific Outline of 1 Timothy:

1. Paul's charge to the assembly of God (*Chapters 1-3*)

   A. The doctrine of the church (*Chapter 1*)
      - His introduction (*1 Timothy 1:1-2*)
        ▶ Paul writes to his child in the faith, Timothy (*1 Timothy 1:1-2*)
        ▶ Paul gives his greeting of grace, mercy and peace (*1 Timothy 1:2*)
      - His warning of false doctrine (*1 Timothy 1:3-11*)
        ▶ The charge to preserve purity of doctrine (*1 Timothy 1:3*)
        ▶ The charge to avoid non-Biblical authorities (*1 Timothy 1:4-7*)
          ▷ They promote doubt, not faith (*1 Timothy 1:4*)
          ▷ They spread confusion, not understanding (*1 Timothy 1:6-7*)
          ▷ They are fruitless and work under false confidence (*1 Timothy 1:6-7*)
        ▶ The charge to minister love and faith, by means of a good conscience (*1 Timothy 1:5*)
        ▶ The proper use of the law (*1 Timothy 1:8-11*)
          ▷ The law still has a useful function (*1 Timothy 1:8*)
          ▷ It is not a way of life for the righteous (*1 Timothy 1:9*)
          ▷ Its use is primarily for the conviction of sinners (*1 Timothy 1:9-11*)
      - His thanks to God for his ministry (*1 Timothy 1:12-17*)
        ▶ He was appointed as faithful by Christ (*1 Timothy 1:12*)
        ▶ He was extended mercy as to his previous life (*1 Timothy 1:13, 14*)
        ▶ His case became an example of God's grace (*1 Timothy 1:15, 16*)
          ▷ Paul demonstrated what the Gospel could do (*1 Timothy 1:15-16*)
          ▷ As chief of sinners, he demonstrated that anyone could be saved (*1 Timothy 1:15-16*)
          ▷ Jesus Christ demonstrated his perfect patience (*1 Timothy 1:16*)
      - His charge to Timothy concerning his gifts (*1 Timothy 1:18-20*)
        ▶ He is able to fully use his own gifts (*1 Timothy 1:18*)
        ▶ He is to war with the weapons of faith (*1 Timothy 1:18*)
        ▶ He is to maintain the faith and a good conscience (*1 Timothy 1:19*)

NOTES

- He is to guard against neglecting his gifts (*1 Timothy 1:19, 20*)
  - Remember that two had suffered shipwreck (*1 Timothy 1:20*)
  - Neglect of either doctrine or conscience can bring shipwreck to your ministry (*1 Timothy 1:19, 20*)

B. The worship in the church (*Chapter 2*)
- The place of prayer in worship (*1 Timothy 2:1-8*)
  - The various aspects of prayer noted (*1 Timothy 2:1*)
  - The objects of prayer (*1 Timothy 2:1-4*)
    - For all men (*1 Timothy 2:1*)
    - For kings and civil leaders (*1 Timothy 2:2*)
    - For the salvation of all (*1 Timothy 2:4*)
  - The Mediator of prayer (*1 Timothy 2:5-7*)
  - The attitude of prayer (*1 Timothy 2:8*)
    - With holy hands lifted up (*1 Timothy 2:8*)
    - Without wrath and dissention (*1 Timothy 2:8*)
- The place of women in worship (*1 Timothy 2:9-15*)
  - Her adornment (*1 Timothy 2:9, 10*)
    - Negatively – not with outward appearances primarily (*1 Timothy 2:9*)
    - Positively – adorned with good character (*1 Timothy 2:10*)
  - Her authority in the church (*1 Timothy 2:11-15*)
- Her place of contribution in the home (*1 Timothy 2:15*)

C. The leaders of the church (*Chapter 3*)
- Qualifications for elders (*1 Timothy 3:1-7*)
  - Desire for work (*1 Timothy 3:1*)
  - Blameless character (*1 Timothy 3:2*)
  - The husband of one wife (*1 Timothy 3:2*)
  - Temperate and prudent (*1 Timothy 3:2*)
  - Respectable and hospitable (*1 Timothy 3:2*)
  - Able to teach (*1 Timothy 3:3*)
  - Not addicted to wine or pugnacious (*1 Timothy 3:3*)
  - Gentle (*1 Timothy 3:3*)
  - Free from the love of money (*1 Timothy 3:3*)
  - A leader of his own household who manages well (*1 Timothy 3:4*)
  - Keeps his children under control with all dignity (*1 Timothy 3:4*)
  - Not a new convert (*1 Timothy 3:6*)
  - A good reputation with unbelievers (*1 Timothy 3:6*)
- Qualifications for deacons (*1 Timothy 3:8-10, 12, 13*)
  - Men of dignity (*1 Timothy 3:8*)
  - Genuine (*1 Timothy 3:8*)
  - Not addicted to much wine (*1 Timothy 3:8*)
  - Not fond of sordid gain (*1 Timothy 3:8*)
  - Strong in the faith with a clear conscience (*1 Timothy 3:9*)
  - The church needs to observe those who display such qualities (*1 Timothy 3:10*)
  - Beyond reproach (*1 Timothy 3:10*)
  - Husband of one wife (*1 Timothy 3:12*)
  - Good managers of their children and household (*1 Timothy 3:12*)

- ▶ Deacons who serve well receive rewards (*1 Timothy 3:13*)
- • Qualifications for female deacons (*1 Timothy 3:11*)
  - ▶ Dignified (*1 Timothy 3:11*)
  - ▶ Not a malicious gossiper (*1 Timothy 3:11*)
  - ▶ Temperate (*1 Timothy 3:11*)
  - ▶ Faithful in all things (*1 Timothy 3:11*)
- • Obligation to promote godliness (*1 Timothy 3:14-16*)
  - ▶ Holiness should characterize God's house (*1 Timothy 3:14-15*)
  - ▶ God's provision for holiness (*1 Timothy 3:16*)
    - ▷ The incarnation of Christ Jesus (*1 Timothy 3:16*)
    - ▷ His vindication in the Spirit (*1 Timothy 3:16*)
    - ▷ He was observed by angels (*1 Timothy 3:16*)
    - ▷ He is preached to all nations (*1 Timothy 3:16*)
    - ▷ He is believed on by many (*1 Timothy 3:16*)
    - ▷ He was received up to be our Intercessor (*1 Timothy 3:16*)

2. Paul's charge to the servant of God (*Chapters 4-6*)

   A. Maintaining godliness in the assembly (*Chapter 4*)
   - • By exposing false doctrine (*1 Timothy 4:1-7*)
     - ▶ The coming apostasy (*1 Timothy 4:1*)
     - ▶ The coming apostates (*1 Timothy 4:2-3*)
       - ▷ They are seduced by Satan (*1 Timothy 4:2-3*)
       - ▷ They are without conscience towards God (*1 Timothy 4:2-3*)
       - ▷ They are often legalistic and ascetic (*1 Timothy 4:2-3*)
     - ▶ God's Word and prayer sanctify all things created by God (*1 Timothy 4:4-5*)
     - ▶ The command for a leader to point out error (*1 Timothy 4:6*)
       - ▷ Concerning legalism, the need for holiness and healthy teachers (*1 Timothy 4:6*)
       - ▷ Their obedience to his command results in spiritual fruitfulness (*1 Timothy 4:6*)
         - ◆ A good servant of Jesus (*1 Timothy 4:6*)
         - ◆ Constantly nourished on the words of the faith and in sound doctrine (*1 Timothy 4:6*)
   - • By exercising godliness (*1 Timothy 4:7-11*)
     - ▶ Avoid worldly fables (*1 Timothy 4:7*)
     - ▶ Discipline yourself for the goal of godliness (*1 Timothy 4:7-8*)
       - ▷ Godly discipline has value here on earth (*1 Timothy 4:8*)
       - ▷ Godly discipline has value for eternity (*1 Timothy 4:8*)
     - ▶ Our work for God centers around the person of God (*1 Timothy 4:9, 10*)
     - ▶ God's servant prescribes and teaches the truths of God (*1 Timothy 4:11*)
   - • By expounding true doctrine (*1 Timothy 4:12-16*)
     - ▶ Be confident of your calling as a leader of God's work (*1 Timothy 4:12*)
       - ▷ Be an example of those who believe (*1 Timothy 4:12*)
       - ▷ Don't despise being young and in ministry (*1 Timothy 4:12*)
     - ▶ Hold fast to the verbal and dynamic ministry of the Word (*1 Timothy 4:13*)

NOTES
- ▶ Exercise and improve your God-given gifts (*1 Timothy 4:14-16*)
  - ▷ Cultivate your gifts (*1 Timothy 4:14*)
  - ▷ Guard your personal life (*1 Timothy 4:15, 16*)
  - ▷ Emphasize your teaching ministry (*1 Timothy 4:16*)
  - ▷ Persevere in ministry (*1 Timothy 4:16*)

B. Maintaining good relationships with all classes (*Chapters 5-6*)
- Treatment of the elderly and younger (*1 Timothy 5:1, 2*)
  - ▶ Treatment of the elderly (*1 Timothy 5:1, 2*)
    - ▷ Don't sharply rebuke an older man (*1 Timothy 5:1*)
    - ▷ Appeal to him as a father (*1 Timothy 5:1*)
    - ▷ Appeal to the older women as mothers (*1 Timothy 5:2*)
  - ▶ Treatment of the younger (*1 Timothy 5:1, 2*)
    - ▷ Appeal to the younger men as brothers (*1 Timothy 5:1*)
    - ▷ Appeal to the younger women as sisters (*1 Timothy 5:2*)

C. Do all of the above in purity
- Treatment of widows who serve (*1 Timothy 5:3-16*)
  - ▶ Widows indeed were a special class without support (*1 Timothy 5:5*)
  - ▶ These widows indeed were to be given special honor (*1 Timothy 5:3*)
  - ▶ These widows indeed were unique servants of prayer (*1 Timothy 5:5*)
  - ▶ Children of widows were first obligated to support the widows (*1 Timothy 5:4*)
  - ▶ Widows given to pleasure were disqualified (*1 Timothy 5:6*)
  - ▶ Widows need to be protected by the church so they may be above reproach (*1 Timothy 5:7*)
  - ▶ This shows one has not denied the faith (*1 Timothy 5:8*)
  - ▶ Qualifications for widows indeed (*1 Timothy 5:9, 10*)
    - ▷ Their age – 60 or over (*1 Timothy 5:9*)
    - ▷ Their marriage – the wife of one man (*1 Timothy 5:9*)
    - ▷ Their ministry of diligence (*1 Timothy 5:10*)
  - ▶ Disqualification of younger widows (*1 Timothy 5:11-13*)
    - ▷ They are likely to remarry (*1 Timothy 5:11-13*)
    - ▷ Their further romance may not incline toward piety (*1 Timothy 5:11, 12*)
    - ▷ To revoke their widow's oath of service would suggest disservice to the work of Christ (*1 Timothy 5:12*)
    - ▷ They use their time poorly (*1 Timothy 5:13*)
  - ▶ Paul's advice to younger widows (*1 Timothy 5:14-16*)
    - ▷ Remarry and bring up children (*1 Timothy 5:14*)
    - ▷ Keep house and alert for the enemies schemes (*1 Timothy 5:14*)
    - ▷ Keep the faith (*1 Timothy 5:15*)
    - ▷ The church needs to support widows indeed (*1 Timothy 5:16*)
- Treatment of ministering elders (*1 Timothy 5:17-25*)
  - ▶ Double honor for those who rule well (*1 Timothy 5:17, 18*)
    - ▷ Ruling well is the qualification (*1 Timothy 5:17*)
    - ▷ All who rule well are worthy of double honor, especially preachers and teachers who work hard are worthy of double honor (*1 Timothy 5:17*)
    - ▷ Do not hinder the progress of the Gospel (*1 Timothy 5:18*)
    - ▷ This principle is seen in the Old Testament (*1 Timothy 5:18*)

- Discipline for erring elders (*1 Timothy 5:19-25*)
  - Be sure evidence of infraction is valid (*1 Timothy 5:19-21*)
  - Invoke discipline as wide as the offense (*1 Timothy 5:20*)
  - Be cautious in appointing leaders (*1 Timothy 5:22, 24, 25*)
    - Great responsibility lies in setting apart people for the ministry (*1 Timothy 5:22*)
    - Be discerning, some sins of individuals are not so obvious (*1 Timothy 5:24, 25*)
    - A parenthesis on wine for medication (*1 Timothy 5:23*)
      - Timothy had been drinking water exclusively for his ailments (*1 Timothy 5:23*)
      - Paul informs the elder he can use wine to a small measure for his stomach and frequent ailments (*1 Timothy 5:23*)
  - Instruction concerning servanthood (*1 Timothy 6:1-6*)
    - Paul's word for servants (*1 Timothy 6:1, 2*)
      - The need to honor masters (*1 Timothy 6:1, 2*)
        - Christian servants should serve well (*1 Timothy 6:1,2*)
        - There should be no revolt (*1 Timothy 6:2*)
      - The reason for honoring masters (*1 Timothy 6:1, 2*)
        - Godly conduct honors God and adorns the Gospel (*1 Timothy 6:1, 2*)
        - Do not take advantage of believing masters (*1 Timothy 6:2*)
    - Paul's word concerning false teachers (*1 Timothy 6:3-5*)
      - They support strange doctrines (*1 Timothy 6:3*)
      - They are identified by nit-picking and strife (*1 Timothy 6:4, 5*)
        - They quibble about minor issues for argumentation (*1 Timothy 6:4*)
        - They are often in it for personal gain (*1 Timothy 6:5*)
  - Instruction concerning wealth (*1 Timothy 6:6-21*)
    - Be content (*1 Timothy 6:6-8*)
      - Contentment is only found in our Lord Jesus (*1 Timothy 6:6-8*)
      - Riches are very temporal (*1 Timothy 6:7, 8*)
    - Covetousness always brings disaster
      - It is the root of all types of evil (*1 Timothy 6:9, 10*)
      - It often leads away from the faith (*1 Timothy 6:10*)
    - Paul's personal charge to the man of God (*1 Timothy 6:11-16*)
      - Flee covetousness and lust (*1 Timothy 6:11*)
      - Follow Godly character qualities (*1 Timothy 6:11*)
      - Fight the good fight of faith (*1 Timothy 6:12*)
      - Fulfill your ministry as unto the Lord (*1 Timothy 6:13, 14*)
        - Christ was undaunted in the face of death before Pilate (*1 Timothy 6:13*)
        - Join the ones who are faithful until He comes again (*1 Timothy 6:14*)
      - Remember the mighty King and Lord whom you serve (*1 Timothy 6:15, 16*)
    - Paul's charge to the rich (*1 Timothy 6:17-19*)

NOTES

- → Beware of the self-sufficiency of riches (*1 Timothy 6:18, 19*)
- → Put your security in God (*1 Timothy 6:17*)
- → Beware of a wrong use of riches (*1 Timothy 6:18, 19*)
  - ↳ Use riches for eternity (*1 Timothy 6:18, 19*)
  - ↳ Using it properly is laying hold of eternal life (*1 Timothy 6:19*)
  - ↳ Demonstrate a giving heart (*1 Timothy 6:18*)
- ◆ Paul's final charge to Timothy (*1 Timothy 6:20-21*)
  - → Guard sound doctrine (*1 Timothy 6:20*)
  - → Defend against false doctrine (*1 Timothy 6:20, 21*)

Chapter Overview:

This first chapter deals with two issues: good doctrine and bad. Good doctrine refers to the Gospel, which was handed down from Paul and the other apostles. It includes the life, teaching, death and resurrection of Jesus. This is the key message of the early church. False doctrine is anything that goes against these core beliefs.

Timothy, as a leader in the church, had to confront false doctrine as well as defend true doctrine. Though Timothy was young, he had the encouragement of Paul to support him.

False doctrine divides churches. The Gospel unites them. Churches are to be united against false doctrine as well as be places that teach the message of salvation in Jesus Christ.

True doctrine makes itself known through the good works of those who believe. False doctrines result in arguments and fights. True doctrine results in love and good works.

One example of false doctrine today is sometimes called "prosperity theology." This means that God will reward obedience with money and possessions. Many people like this idea, because it means that becoming a part of the ministry will help you get rich. This is not what the Gospel teaches. Jesus must be our greatest treasure. Those in the ministry must stand against these false doctrines and live their lives based on the truths of God's Word.

Commentary:

A. Paul's salutation (*1 Timothy 1:1-2*)
- Paul writes to his child in the faith, Timothy (*1 Timothy 1:1-2*)
  - ▶ Paul writes as though under a "Commander." The Romans used to refer to their Emperor as "Savior God." But for Paul, God is the one true God, who must be obeyed.
  - ▶ Paul calls Jesus "our hope." Jesus' death and resurrection provide believers with hope.
  - ▶ Ephesus was a tough place to minister. Therefore it would have been encouraging to hear from Paul. Calling him "a true son" was a sign of love and respect.

- ▶ Timothy was the one to whom the letter was addressed, though in the first century church the letter would have been read aloud before the congregation.
- Paul gives his greeting of grace, mercy and peace (*1 Timothy 1:2*)
  - ▶ Such greetings were customary in the letters of the ancient world. Paul uses a similar format in many other letters (various terms are used in *Romans 1:7, 1 Corinthians 1:3, 2 Corinthians 1:2, Ephesians 1:2, Philippians 1:2* and *Colossians 1:2*).
  - ▶ Paul's desire is that Timothy be blessed, citing specific characteristics of God: "grace, mercy and peace."

B. His warning of false doctrine (*1 Timothy 1:3-11*)
- The charge to preserve purity of doctrine (*1 Timothy 1:3*).
  - ▶ Ephesus was a difficult city to minister in. No one would blame Timothy for wanting to leave. Paul encourages him to stay for the purpose of confronting false teachers.
  - ▶ The "strange doctrines" are hard to define. Paul doesn't describe them. Some suggest these were men practicing a belief called "Gnosticism," but this was not a <u>fully developed</u> belief system until the second century. One commentator writes: "They may have had a Gnostic flavor, but were more likely of Jewish origin (*Titus 1:14*). Whatever their nature, they were empty of any spiritual value and led only to further speculations and arguments."[3]
- The charge to avoid non-Biblical authorities (*1 Timothy 1:4-7*).
  - ▶ They promote doubt, not faith (*1 Timothy 1:4*).
    - ▷ The false teachings did not lead to faith in Jesus and the Gospel, but only doubt and speculation.
    - ▷ Speculations are "to be avoided because they did not further God's plan, which is grasped and implemented not by human imaginings, but by faith."[4]
  - ▶ They minister confusion, not understanding (*1 Timothy 1:6-7*).
    - ▷ False teachers fail to achieve love and faith, and rely on clever words and ideas: "human speculations tend to lead off down endless blind tunnels which serve only to confuse and obscure God's truth."[5]
    - ▷ "Idle chatter" is a key feature of false teachers in the Pastoral Letters.
    - ▷ Those who do not love God's Truth do not respect the cross. This is why Paul says in *1 Corinthians 1:18*:
      - ◆ "*For the message of the cross is foolishness to those who are perishing, but to us who are being saved it is the power of God.*"
    - ▷ In Philippians, Paul warns of those who are "enemies of the cross:" *Philippians 3:18-19*:
      - ◆ "*For many walk, of whom I have told you often, and now tell you even weeping, that they are the enemies of the cross of Christ: whose end is destruction, whose god is their belly, and whose glory is in their shame—who set their mind on earthly things.*"
- Paul is warning that those who practice false doctrine are known for immorality and "idle chatter."

NOTES

- They are fruitless and work under false confidence (*1 Timothy 1:6-7*).
  - The false teachers wanted to be respected as good teachers of the Old Testament Law. But what they were really after was respect, because they were consumed with pride in themselves rather than love for people.
  - The false teachers were over confident, but did not understand what they were teaching.
- The charge to minister love and faith, by means of a good conscience (*1 Timothy 1: 5*).
  - Godly instruction leads to love. God's workers always have this as the ultimate goal.
  - Love comes from "a pure heart, a good conscience and a sincere faith." Unlike the false teachers, love seeks to serve others rather than to be served by others.
  - "Each member of this beautiful trio speaks of a purity and integrity which produces the most exquisite kind of selfless love, seen in its ultimate form in God's love itself. Whereas the false teachers were motivated by worthless curiosity, Paul's instruction was designed to promote the most magnificent of virtues by maintaining the purity of the church's teaching. God's truth always purifies the human spirit, while error [corrupts] it."[6]
- The proper use of the law (*1 Timothy 1:8-11*).
  - The law still has a useful function (*1 Timothy 1:8*).
    - The law was good when used properly.
    - The law was bad when inappropriately used to promote legalism – teaching that Christians had to follow the law to be saved (*Galatians 3:19, 24*).
  - It is not a way of life for the righteous (*1 Timothy 1:9*).
    - The purpose of the law was to reveal sinfulness, but it was not meant to be the Christian way of life.
    - Christians are no longer under the law but walk by the Spirit.
  - Its use is primarily for the conviction of sinners (*1 Timothy 1:9-11*).
    - This list of qualities differs from the love in *verse 5*.
    - The qualities listed here seem to resemble the Ten Commandments. The false teachers wanted to teach the law, but they weren't even living by the law.
    - Only immoral living can produce such rotten teaching.
    - Sound doctrine is found in the Gospel, which is a great treasure with which Timothy has been entrusted.[7]

Questions

How have you had to deal with false doctrine?

Discuss together different ways of handling false teachings inside and outside of the Church.

NOTES

Chapter Two
1 Timothy 1:12-20

Chapter Overview:

Sound doctrine reveals itself in the life of those who teach it. The greatest witness to unbelievers is a life that reflects the hope of Christ Jesus.

Jesus was and is the example of love and obedience. Those who place their faith in Him will show this same love and obedience in their own lives. Good doctrine leads to humility. False teachers are known for being prideful, which often produces arguing and fighting. Those who follow Jesus must respond to these false teachings with faithful obedience and Christian love, following after the One who taught us to pray for those who persecute us.

Christian leaders must persevere. The false teachings will often look very appealing, and many in the church may turn aside from God's Truth to follow after these teachings. Christian leaders must remain faithful to the Truth in order not to fall away into the traps of these false teachings, which often lead to arguments and immorality.

Commentary:

A. His thanks to God for his ministry (*1 Timothy 1:12-17*)
   - He was appointed as faithful by Christ (*1 Timothy 1:12*)
     ▶ Christ alone provides the strength for ministry.
     ▶ God regarded Paul as trustworthy. There is no higher goal in ministry then to meet God's approval. We meet this approval by remaining faithful to the Gospel.
     ▶ In Galatians, Paul says that he received the Gospel directly from God, not from human wisdom. Therefore Paul places high value on us passing on this message to the church.
     ▶ Those whom God regards as trustworthy are entrusted with the Gospel (*1 Timothy 1:11*)
     ▶ Therefore, ministry is a gift, never a burden. Paul is grateful for this call to service.
   - He was extended mercy as to his unregenerate life (*1 Timothy 1:13, 14*)
     ▶ Paul describes his former life as a persecutor of the church (*Acts 9*)
     ▶ The fact that God would use him now is a testimony to God's grace and mercy. While Paul was ignorant, God was gracious and gave him faith. In Corinthians Paul calls himself the "least of the apostles." (*1 Corinthians 15:8*)
     ▶ The source of this grace and love is Jesus Christ. While we were faithless, He died for us. (*Romans 5:7-8*).
   - His case became an example of God's grace (*1 Timothy 1:15-16*)
     ▶ Paul exemplified what the Gospel could do (*1 Timothy 1:15-16*)

- ▷ Jesus came to save the lost sinners.
- ▷ This truth is "trustworthy," meaning that this statement is a fact that can be accepted, unlike the "strange doctrines" of the false teachers.
- ▶ As chief of sinners, he demonstrated that anyone could be saved (*1 Timothy 1:15-16*)
    - ▷ Paul again makes reference to his past. He was the greatest of all sinners. "In *1 Corinthians 15:9* he had called himself 'the least of the apostles...' In *Ephesians 3:8* he refers to himself as 'the less than the least of all saints'... On occasion Paul would defend himself as on par with the twelve apostles and superior to the Judaizers. It is not mock humility here, but sincere appreciation of the sins of his life as a persecutor of the church of God, of men and even women. He has sad memories of those days." [8]
    - ▷ But this violent past only makes God's grace all the more powerful – even the very worst human being can receive the gift of God's grace.
- ▶ Jesus Christ demonstrated his perfect patience (*1 Timothy 1:16*)
    - ▷ If even a former persecutor like Paul can be saved, there's hope for all of us. "The ultimate sinner became the ultimate saint; God's greatest enemy became His finest servant... In studying Paul's pattern Christians can therefore learn about themselves." [9]
    - ▷ This salvation is based on the Christ. Since Christ is equal with God He is able to practice perfect patience.
    - ▷ Therefore, we all can trust in Christ for our salvation.
    - ▷ Like Paul, we can worship God for His grace.

B. His charge to Timothy concerning his gifts (*1 Timothy 1:18-20*)
   - He is able to exploit to the full his own gifts (*1 Timothy 1:18*)
     - ▶ Paul changes from praise of God to commands for Timothy. Timothy was specially "entrusted" with gifts for the ministry, including prophecies. Timothy was to remember these gifts and be inspired by them to persevere.
     - ▶ Paul again calls Timothy "my son." Though they were not physically together, Paul expresses genuine love for his fellow servant.
   - He is to war with the weapons of faith (*1 Timothy 1:18*)
     - ▶ The prophecies Paul mentions also mean that Timothy is encouraged to be a powerful fighter for the sake of the Gospel and against these false teachings.
     - ▶ The military terms reflect Paul's understanding that these false teaching are part of a larger, spiritual war.
     - ▶ In *Ephesians 6:10-18*, we learn that the Christian life is a spiritual war. God's leaders must be equipped for this spiritual battle.
   - He is to maintain the faith and a good conscience (*1 Timothy 1:19*)
     - ▶ Like *verse 5*, the goal is not only to fight against false teachings, but to value personal purity.
     - ▶ Some may become "shipwrecked." This means that it is easy to put aside these qualities and reject God's ways. To reject one's faith and conscience always results in destruction.
   - He is to guard against neglecting his gifts (*1 Timothy 1:19-20*)

NOTES

- ▶ Remember that two men had suffered shipwreck (*1 Timothy 1:20*)
  - ▷ Paul mentions two examples of people who were "shipwrecked." Shipwrecked is a figure of speech meaning they strayed from sound doctrine and wrecked their faith. In *2 Timothy* Hymenaeus is spoken of as having "a mouth that spread like gangrene," meaning that he spread gossip and was quick to spread false teaching and argue. Alexander was a coppersmith who did not repent of sinful behavior. Paul knew that the Lord would bring discipline to them both.
  - ▷ Being "delivered over to Satan" means to be removed or "excommunicated" from the church. This practice was to expose their sin and discipline them so that they might repent.
- ▶ Neglect of either doctrine or conscience can bring shipwreck to your ministry (*1 Timothy 1:19, 20*). Though in the sea of faith, knowing and following Christ Jesus, one can get off course and crash spiritually.[10]

Chapter Three
1 Timothy 2:1-8

Godly leaders seek an extensive prayer life and promote an atmosphere
of prayer and worship in the assembly
(*1 Timothy 2:1-8*)

Chapter Overview:

Christian leaders must possess discipline. Discipline means that godly leaders take joy in daily devoting themselves to God and His ministry by praying, reading the Bible and serving others. It is helpful to set time aside each day to pray and read the Bible.

The church is meant to have this same life of prayer and worship. A healthy church is one that finds joy in worshiping God. The false teachers were selfish and taught false doctrine in order to promote themselves. God's people seek Him alone.

Godly worship is done in purity. Unlike the false teachers who were motivated by pride, godly worship seeks God alone.

Commentary:

   A. The various aspects and objects of prayer (*1 Timothy 2:1-8*)
   - For all men (*1 Timothy 2:1*)
     - Prayer is to be made on behalf of all men. We are to "pray without ceasing." (*1 Thessalonians 5:17*)
     - How should we pray?
       - Entreaties: Praying for God to address specific needs, such as financial needs or needs for healing. The focus is on the fact that only God can meet these needs, and only if it is in His will.
       - Prayer: Prayer that focuses solely on God. "It is through prayer we center our attention on the Lord so we can begin to see ourselves and our circumstances from his perspective... When we see things as he does, we can find an inner rest and joy even in the midst of turmoil and sorrow."[11]
       - Petitions: Prayer that brings us close to God on behalf of someone else. The image here is of going before a King to ask his blessing for someone else. God desires to be close to us and longs for us to depend on Him.
       - Thanksgiving: Prayer that thanks and praises God for the blessings He has given. This type of prayer is an act of worship before God.
   - For kings and civil leaders (*1 Timothy 2:2*)
     - Paul had just been released from prison. He knew better than anyone that the government was in need of God's help.
     - Therefore all Christians are to pray for their government, their leaders and anyone else in authority over them.

- In *Romans 13*, Paul says that leaders are appointed by God. (*Romans 13:1-7*) Therefore we must respect and honor ruling authorities.
- The purpose was so that they could live peacefully with all men.
- For the salvation of all (*1 Timothy 2:4*)
  - The second purpose of prayer was so that all men (including members of the government) might come to know Christ.
  - God is pleased when we pray in this manner.
  - "Knowledge of the truth" refers to come to know Jesus. It is a term Paul uses often to refer to salvation.
  - Not everyone will be saved, but God wants everyone to be saved.

B. The Mediator of prayer (*1 Timothy 2:5-7*)
  - Christ is the "Mediator" of prayer. This means that through Christ we have access to God in prayer.
    - Jesus taught His disciples to pray "in His name."(*John 15:16*)
    - This means praying in a way that reflects your love of Jesus and certainly praying in His character.
  - Paul explains the truth of the Gospel:
    - There is one God.
    - There is one Mediator – Jesus
    - Jesus died on the cross for sin. A "ransom" was a price paid to release a slave (*Mark 10:45*).
    - This happened at the proper time – meaning that Christ's death occurred as part of God's plan.
  - Paul's ministry was in response to this message.
    - The words "for this" mean that since Jesus had given His life for others, so Paul would be willing to give His life for others.
    - Paul was "appointed" by God for this task.
    - To be a "preacher" meant to carry Good News. For Paul this was the Gospel.
    - To be an "apostle" means to be sent forth. As a "preacher" he was to preach the Good News of the Gospel. As an "apostle" he was to carry this news to all men, both Jew and Gentile (*Matthew 28:19-20*).

C. The attitude of prayer (*1 Timothy 2:8*)
  - With holy hands lifted up (*1 Timothy 2:8*)
    - Men were the ones responsible for leading their church in prayer.
    - In the first century, lifting up your hands was common in worship – even non-Christians did this in pagan practices. The idea was to show "holy hands," that is, "clean hands." Lifting one's hands was meant to show one's purity before a Holy God.
  - Without wrath and dissension (*1 Timothy 2:8*)
    - These men were meant to have healthy, loving relationships. Fighting and arguing would weaken God's reputation in the church as well as to those outside it.
    - All believers are called to pray. While these men are to lead the church, prayer is something all believers are meant to practice.[12]

Chapter Four
1 Timothy 2:9-15

Biblical leaders clarify and promote the role of women in the local church
(*1 Timothy 2:9-15*)

Chapter Overview:

Men and women are both created in the image of God. Therefore, all women are equal in the eyes of God. Men are not better than women, nor are women better than men. But though they are equal, they are given different roles to fill. This chapter focuses on the roles women fill in the church.

Women are to show their love of God through their moral character, not their outward beauty. Some women are tempted to think that their greatest virtue is to be beautiful. But Paul makes clear that the most valuable thing about a woman is her moral character.

Women are to participate in church services, but they are not to disrupt them. In some cultures, women are not well educated, and must wait to receive instruction at later times.

In the first century, women were not treated as well as men. In this chapter, we see that Paul wanted to give women a place within the church and allow them to be treated with love and respect.

Commentary:

A. The place of women in worship (*1 Timothy 2:9-10*)
- Her adornment (*1 Timothy 2:9-10*)
    - ▶ Negatively – not primarily with outward appearances (*1 Timothy 2:9*)
        - ▷ The verse begins with the word "likewise." The men had received instruction on their conduct in worship. Now the women were receiving their instruction.
        - ▷ Women were to wear "proper" clothing in worship and to be modest. The issue was pride. Women often wore expensive clothing to show their status. Some churches still sadly see this today.
            - ◆ In Ephesus, temple prostitutes were known by the way they dressed. Women were to avoid dressing in ways that resemble these prostitutes.
            - ◆ Among Jews and Gentiles, "braided hair" was considered a sign of wealth and status.
            - ◆ Gold and pearls were the most expensive items in Ephesus, worn as jewelry or even placed in the hair.
            - ◆ "Costly garments" refers to expensive clothing. Both women and men were known for wearing fine clothing as a way of showing off their great wealth and success.

- "Modestly" and "discreetly" both refer to sexual matters. Women were to avoid clothing that was overly revealing or sexually enticing. This often varies from culture to culture, but women usually know when their clothing is not modest.
- Positively – adorned with good character (*1 Timothy 2:10*)
  - Women are not to impress others by their clothing, but through their godly character.
  - Good works are "proper" for women in the church, because their lives should reflect the righteousness of God.

B. Her authority in the church (*1 Timothy 2:11-15*)
- Women are to quietly receive instruction.
  - Women in the first century were less educated than men, and were more likely to disrupt meetings with questions or incorrect statements (*1 Corinthians 14:34*).
  - Women were meant to learn, but with "quiet instruction." This at times meant waiting until after the church meeting to ask questions about what she didn't understand.
- Women are not permitted to teach or have authority over men.
  - In Ephesus, false teachers were using women to spread their false teachings.
  - Women are not permitted to teach men or have authority over them. This means that they would not be permitted to be pastors or elders.
  - They can teach and preach the Word of God with the approval of the elders.
- The roles of women are based on creation.
  - Some would say these rules are based only on Paul's culture. But Paul makes clear that these roles are based on the created order:
    - Adam was made first
    - Eve was made second
    - Adam named Eve, showing his authority over her.
  - Adam and Eve were both created "in the image of God." (*Genesis 1:26*) They were both equal. They simply had different roles.
  - Woman was deceived in the beginning. Now they were being deceived again by false teachers. These rules were set in place to protect women and the church from being deceived by false teaching. However, we must remember that God values the teaching of women so much that they are the ones who are home often more than the men to train the young boys and girls in the house.

C. Her place of contribution in the home (*1 Timothy 2:15*)
- A woman's role was primarily in the household.
- Being a mother was a high calling, and not a task to avoid in favor of being a leader in the church.
- Women could still have a role in the church as deacons (*1 Timothy 3:11*).
- Women were considered a valuable part of the church community.
- Like men, women were expected to possess godly qualities:
  - "Dignified" (*1 Timothy 2:11*): this word means worthy of respect. It probably refers not only to modest dress, but refers to her godly character as well.

NOTES

NOTES

- Not a malicious gossiper (*1 Timothy 2:11*): women were not to put others down through their words. Loving others meant showing respect to everyone in the church community.
- Temperate (*1 Timothy 2:11*): this meant that she was fair and balanced, not given to anger or arguments.
- Faithful in all things (*1 Timothy 2:11*): the woman was to be faithfully committed to her tasks. This included both her commitments to the church as well as her commitments in the home.[13]

Questions

What roles can women play in your new church?

How will you look to involve women in the different aspects of the ministry of church planting?

Chapter Five
1 Timothy 3:1-7

Chapter Overview:

Church ministry is an important responsibility, therefore church leaders must be chosen based on God's standards of maturity and integrity.

This chapter lists the qualifications that church leaders must possess. An elder was to have the same qualities as a pastor; therefore their lives must show their faithfulness to God's message and God's righteous character.

Though elders were meant to be humble, this position was something that people could desire to have. It is a good thing when Christians desire to serve. Christian leaders should be encouraged when others come to them and want to serve in the church. Their lives must then be looked at to see if they meet God's standards for ministry.

Commentary:

A. Qualifications for elders (*1 Timothy 3:1-7*)
- Desire for the work (*1 Timothy 3:1*)
  - To be an elder is a great responsibility.
  - "Elder" and "bishop" refer to the same role.
  - It is a good thing for someone to want to have this role. But it is also a position of great sacrifice that must be taken seriously.
- Blameless character (*1 Timothy 3:2*)
  - The elder is to be "above reproach." This doesn't mean "perfect," but it means that the elder strives to live a life of moral integrity.
  - Blameless character is further described in the qualities listed in *1 Timothy 3:2-7*.
- The husband of one wife (*1 Timothy 3:2*)
  - The verse literally means "a one woman man." This means that the man is committed to his wife and not involved with another woman.
  - This doesn't mean that you have to be married. But single men must also display sexual integrity by not looking for sexual satisfaction outside of marriage.
  - There is a great debate regarding the issue of divorce.
    - Some say elders who divorce and remarry cannot be elders.
    - Others say that there must be a long time before the man can serve again as an elder if divorced or divorced and remarried.
    - Still others say that elders can remarry after their wives die.
    - The message of this verse is the normal, desirable condition for an elder. While these issues are matters of concern, they do not change the clear instruction that elders are to be faithful to their wives.
- Temperate and prudent (*1 Timothy 3:2*)

- ▶ "Temperate" means to be well *balanced* and not given to anger or outbursts of emotion.
- ▶ "Prudent" refers to being self-controlled and able to apply God's Truth.
- ▶ Elders must possess these qualities because of the great temptation to make decisions based on emotion rather than on God's Truth.
- Respectable and hospitable (*1 Timothy 3:2*)
  - ▶ "Respectable" means to be "a consistent man... able to work through even the toughest of problems, with clear, wise and decisive thinking."[14]
  - ▶ "Hospitable" means to be friendly and willing to welcome people into his home. They must be willing to talk and spend time with people.
- Able to teach (*1 Timothy 3:3*)
  - ▶ An elder may not have the gift of teaching, but he should still be able to teach God's truth and defend sound doctrine. All Christians should be able to explain the Bible as they grow and mature. (*Hebrews 5:14*).
  - ▶ This ability is different from false teachers. A true man of God will display what he's teaching in the way he lives his life and conducts his ministry.
- Not addicted to wine (*1 Timothy 3:3*)
  - ▶ "Addicted to wine" refers to someone who is controlled by his desire for alcohol. An elder is to display self-control. Wine was not forbidden, but it was to be consumed in moderation.
  - ▶ "Pugnacious" means being someone who gets into fights and starts violence. This means not hitting his wife and kids, as well as not fighting others in the church or city.
  - ▶ Alcohol can lead to violence: *Proverbs 20:1, "Wine is a mocker, Strong drink is a brawler, and whoever is led astray by it is not wise."*
- Gentle and uncontentious (*1 Timothy 3:3*)
  - ▶ "Gentle" means to be patient and kind with others, even those with whom he disagrees.
  - ▶ "Uncontentious" means to not be a fighter or prone to argue.
  - ▶ The elder must be kind and sensitive to others, avoiding arguments.
- Free from the love of money (*1 Timothy 3:3*)
  - ▶ God will bless those in ministry, but this doesn't always mean the blessing is financial. Elders are to avoid the trap of greed.
  - ▶ The love of money is a snare that leads only to a spiritual fall. It's not that money is evil, but that our hearts desire money instead of desiring to be servants of God.
  - ▶ Jesus warned that you can't serve two masters – God and money (*Matthew 6:24*). A church leader must be fully devoted to God.
- A manager of his own household who manages well (*1 Timothy 3:4*)
  - ▶ An elder must be a leader in his home as well as in the church. This doesn't mean running the home like a business, but for his family (wife, children and those living under his roof), to follow his leadership with love.
  - ▶ *Titus 1:6* mentions the elder is to have "children who believe." The elder is expected to have children who share their father's love for the Lord. This does not mean the elder is responsible for their spirituality. Even the most devout parents can have children who do not

believe or who later choose to rebel from the faith. But it means the elder should conduct his household so that it encourages belief in God.
- Keeps his children under control with all dignity (*1 Timothy 3:4*)
    - ▶ The elder treats his children with respect.
    - ▶ The elder's children are expected to not be out of control or demonstrate immoral behavior. As before, the elder is not directly responsible for his children's behavior, but should conduct himself and household in a way that is honoring to God and serves as an example for his children.
- Not a new convert (*1 Timothy 3:6*)
    - ▶ New believers cannot be expected to have the experience and maturity necessary for leading a church.
    - ▶ New believers are in most direct danger of being taken in by the false teachings, since they do not have the experience to understand good and false doctrine.
- A good reputation with unbelievers (*1 Timothy 3:6*)
    - ▶ "Those outside the church" refers to those who do not believe.
        - ▷ Unbelievers look at Christians closely, trying to see if their conduct matches what they believe. Falling into "reproach" means to lose this good reputation with the outside world. Christians must show outsiders that their beliefs produce good character.
        - ▷ *In Colossians 4:5-6, Paul teaches to "Walk in wisdom toward those who are outside, redeeming the time. Let your speech always be with grace, seasoned with salt, that you may know how you ought to answer each one."* Our lives should be living examples of who we serve.
        - ▷ There is a danger that Christians can become removed from the culture they seek to reach. Christians are called to witness to unbelievers, in the hopes that they come to know Jesus.
    - ▶ The other danger is falling into the "snare of the devil." The Devil does not want God's church to succeed. The best way for the church to fail is for it to have a bad reputation with the outside world through immoral living.

B. Reflections on the office
- In the home: the elder's home reflects his character. The elder must view his family as a part of his ministry, treating his family with love and honor, and encouraging his family's spiritual development.
- Personally: The elder must also be a man of moral integrity. His life should reflect the God he claims to follow.
- In the church: The elder must be a leader in the church. Therefore they need to be men of godly character, and able to lead the people with wisdom and gentleness.
- Socially: Both Christians and unbelievers should have a respect for the elder. His life should draw others closer to God. He must be friendly with others as well as display good moral character.
- Spiritually: Elders draw strength from God. This means an ongoing life of prayer, study and devotion. These practices will be revealed in the elder's lifestyle, as his good works reflect his beliefs.

C. Rewards of the ministry
- Eternal treasures: Ministry is hard. Often there are few rewards here on earth. Some have said that if you obey God, he will bless you with money and wealth here on earth. But the elder understands that ministry on earth is difficult. Elders who lead well are promised rewards in heaven. Therefore, ministry is not about seeking wealth or status, but about pursuing God's Kingdom.
- Joy and satisfaction: Though ministry is hard, it can also bring joy and satisfaction, even when facing difficulty. Joy and satisfaction do not come from money, possessions or even health – some men have given their lives and still been filled with joy. Joy and satisfaction come from remaining faithful to God and leading the church.
- Growth and maturity: As the elder leads others, he experiences spiritual growth in his own life. This is why Jesus speaks of God's Kingdom as a storehouse. The elder develops his own character, and others receive the benefit of this labor.[15]

Question

Do you fit the qualifications of an elder? If not, what areas do you need to work on strengthening? Discuss with others.

Chapter Six
1 Timothy 3:8-13

Chapter Overview:

Elders and deacons are different positions. Elders serve Jesus by leading the local church; deacons serve Jesus by ministering for and to the elders and the local church. Elders are only men, but deacons can be men or women.

Deacons were held to the same basic moral standards as elders. This chapter goes into detail regarding the qualifications for deacons.

All church leaders are defined by being a servant. Jesus was the greatest Servant of all. Those who follow Him will follow His example by becoming a humble servant. As before, the false teachers were looking for position and status in the church because of their pride. Godly leaders are humble and live a life of love and service.

Commentary:

- A. Qualifications for deacons (*1 Timothy 3:8-10, 12, 13*)
  - Men or Women of dignity (*1 Timothy 3:8*)
    - ▶ The word "likewise" means that just as elders had certain qualities, so too should deacons.
    - ▶ "Dignity" means to be stable. He is worthy of respect. While this doesn't mean he can't laugh and enjoy himself, a person cannot have dignity if he is always making jokes and refuses to take things seriously.
  - Genuine (*1 Timothy 3:8*)
    - ▶ "Not double tongued" means that he is honest. He is not saying one thing to one person, and something different to another. He cannot say one thing while thinking another. He tells the truth openly to others.
    - ▶ The deacon is the same person regardless of where he is. He treats his family with the same respect he treats those at church.
  - Not addicted to much wine (*1 Timothy 3:8*)
    - ▶ Like elders, deacons are not to become dependent on alcohol.
    - ▶ Alcohol affects one's judgment. Care must be taken so that alcohol does not damage one's love of God. For many, this might mean not drinking any alcohol.
  - Not fond of sordid gain (*1 Timothy 3:8*)
    - ▶ "Sordid gain" means chasing after money. The word "sordid" means immoral. Believers must not become greedy, or try to benefit from others. This can mean not taking bribes and not pursuing wealth to the neglect of the church.
    - ▶ God wants to be our sole desire. He will not tolerate men who replace Him with money or possessions. Ministers may feel tempted to pursue material wealth by entering the ministry or serving in the

church. But the greatest treasure of all is God's gracious gift of His Son. Money is therefore of lesser importance and should not be pursued.

- Strong in the faith with a clear conscience (*1 Timothy 3:9*)
  - ▶ The "mystery" of the faith refers to the central belief in the life, death and resurrection of Jesus. To "hold" these beliefs is to treat them as you would a valuable treasure.
  - ▶ A "pure" or "clear conscience" means to remain pure. It means to practice God's commands here on earth, and to live a life consistent with what you believe.
- The church needs to observe those who display such qualities (*1 Timothy 3:10*)
  - ▶ "Tested" means that a person's life is looked at closely and seen to match the character of God. This probably doesn't mean an actual "test," but an observation of the way the person conducts his life over time as they live their lives and are involved in ministry.
  - ▶ This also means that this person's character is looked at before becoming a deacon. Therefore, the person is observed as a servant before being given the title.
- Beyond reproach (*1 Timothy 3:10*)
  - ▶ Like the elders, deacons are to be men and women of moral integrity.
  - ▶ The phrase "beyond reproach" covers all of the qualities mentioned for both elders and deacons. It is therefore a summary statement of all qualities.
- Husband of one wife (*1 Timothy 3:12*)
  - ▶ See Chapter 4 for an explanation of *1 Timothy 3:11*.
  - ▶ Like the elders, the deacon is to be sexually pure. This means that married deacons must remain faithful to their wives/husbands, and singles must not pursue sexual satisfaction outside of marriage.
- Good managers of their children and household (*1 Timothy 3:12*)
  - ▶ The household is the primary area where leadership is displayed. The leadership they practice in the home is a model for the leadership they practice in the church.
  - ▶ As with elders, the deacon is expected to have a household of moral integrity and Christian discipleship. The deacon is expected to be a spiritual leader and moral example for his family.
- Deacons who serve well receive rewards (*1 Timothy 3:13*)
  - ▶ Deacons will be rewarded in heaven for their service on earth. The key word is "serving." Church ministry is not about rewards. It is about serving others as Christ did.
  - ▶ Deacons can still expect to see some earthly rewards.
    - ▷ "High standing:" this phrase means "deep respect." Other believers will respect servants of God, even though they may not always be respected by the world.
    - ▷ "Great confidence:" the servant of God will grow in their confidence, feeling bold in their ability to serve others and serve God.

NOTES

"Though the position of deacon seems by worldly standards to be menial and unattractive, to close followers of Jesus Christ it looks quite different. Those who fulfill their servant roles faith-

NOTES

fully gain two things: first, an excellent standing before fellow Christians who understand and appreciate the beauty of humble, selfless, Christlike service; and second, great assurance...in their faith in Christ Jesus. Humble service, which lacks all the rewards the world deems important, becomes a true test of one's motives. Here one discovers for himself whether or not his efforts are truly prompted by a Christlike spirit of selfless service."[16]

- B. The office of deacon in perspective
  - Our Lord's emphasis on servanthood
    - ▶ Jesus was the ultimate Servant:
      - ▷ *Matthew 20:27-28, "And whoever desires to be first among you, let him be your slave —s just as the Son of Man did not come to be served, but to serve, and to give His life a ransom for many."*
      - ▷ *Matthew 19:30, "But many who are first will be last, and the last first."*
      - ▷ *Mark 9:35, "If anyone desires to be first, he shall be last of all and servant of all."*
    - ▶ Therefore the life of the deacon (or any servant of God) is meant to follow this example. The life of a Christian servant is not about rewards or glory, but about humble obedience to others, and following after the character of Jesus.
  - Ways to encourage deacons.
    - ▶ Thank the deacons in your church. Writing a simple letter can be very encouraging to them.
    - ▶ Ask for their advice or help in some area. This will give them a chance to serve you, which is something servants of God are glad to do.[17]

Question

How will you teach the qualifications of deacons in your new church? Are you working on raising up other leaders to also go and plant churches? Discuss.

NOTES

CHAPTER SEVEN
1 TIMOTHY 5:1-2

Biblical leaders maintain healthy social and personal relationships
(*1 Timothy 5:1-2*)

Chapter Overview:

The church is the body of Christ. It is also a family. The relationships we have in the church must resemble the love and respect of relationships in one's family.

Older Christians are to be treated as parents. This means respecting them and listening to them. Just as our mothers and fathers have advice to share, so do older Christians. Older Christians often have wisdom and experience that younger believers may benefit from. These people are therefore a valuable part of God's family.

Likewise, younger Christians are to be treated as siblings. As brothers and sisters, younger Christians must receive love and respect. This helps to avoid sexual temptation with younger women. Treating young men as brothers helps provide leadership for the coming generations in the church.

Commentary:

- A. Treatment of the elderly and younger (*1 Timothy 5:1-2*)
  - Treatment of the elderly (*1 Timothy 5:1-2*)
    - ▶ Don't sharply rebuke an older man (*1 Timothy 5:1*)
      - ▷ "Sharply rebuke" means to be unkind and disrespectful to the old. Older Christians often have experience and wisdom to contribute to churches that must be heard and given respect.
      - ▷ An "older man" refers to older men in the church, not necessarily an elder or church leader.
    - ▶ Appeal to him as a father (*1 Timothy 5:1*)
      - ▷ Instead of being harsh with the older men, Timothy is given instruction to treat them with kindness and encouragement.
      - ▷ Timothy is told to treat older men as he would his own father. Christians are a part of God's family, and should treat all family members with respect. In this verse, we should treat those older than us with the respect we give to our parents.
    - ▶ Appeal to the older women as mothers (*1 Timothy 5:2*)
      - ▷ Likewise, Christians are to treat older women as mothers.
      - ▷ A mother's heart will find joy in gentleness and comfort. Christians are wise to treat older women with love and respect.
  - Treatment of the younger (*1 Timothy 5:1-2*)
    - ▶ Appeal to the younger men as brothers (*1 Timothy 5:1*)
      - ▷ Timothy was a young man. He also had a lot of responsibility as leader of a church in the city of Ephesus. It may have been that other young men were jealous of his position.

- ▷ Timothy was to treat them like he would his own brothers. This meant with respect and love, not responding to any of their jealousy.
- ▷ A good reason to respect these young men is so that they might become strong leaders in the church. As church leaders grow older, they will need to find young Christians to grow to take their place. Young men are the ones who will grow in Christian maturity to one day take the lead within their church.

▶ Appeal to the younger women as sisters (*1 Timothy 5:2*)
- ▷ Likewise, Timothy is told to treat the young women in the church as sisters.
- ▷ The charge to be pure is important. To treat a young woman as a sister means to avoid sexual temptation. There will be a natural temptation to become too involved with a young woman. To treat them as a family member means to respect and love them as a sister and not give in to sexual temptation.[18]

NOTES

Chapter Eight
1 Timothy 5:17-20

Godly leaders take responsibility to promote good financial stewardship
(*1 Timothy 5:17-20*)

Chapter Overview:

Good service deserves to be rewarded. Servants of God give up much in order to serve others. The church must take care to meet the material needs of these men, so that they may continue to serve well.

Service to God is not for the purpose of financial gain, but for God's glory. A church leader does not serve for the purpose of gaining a reward, but out of love of God and love for the church.

Sin must be dealt with within the church. A group of people must be used in dealing with sin, and the church body must understand that sin is taken very seriously. If the sinner is rebuked, the purpose is not to punish him, but to encourage him to repent and turn back to God so that he can become part of the church once more.

Commentary:

A. Double honor for those who rule well (*1 Timothy 5:17-18*)
   - Ruling well is the qualification (*1 Timothy 5:17*)
     ▶ All leaders are called to lead with excellence. This doesn't mean "perfection," but means that leaders devote themselves fully to the task of the ministry. *Colossians 3:23* reminds us that all work is to be performed with excellence because all work is for God's glory.
     ▶ The verse uses the word "elders," which means more than one. Church ministry is a group effort. It takes the skills and gifts of a team of people. Elders are not called to be ministers alone. They are called to serve others with other men and women (deacons) with whom they have relationships.
   - Preachers and teachers who work hard are worthy of double honor (*1 Timothy 5:17*)
     ▶ "Double honor" means extra pay. In the first century, soldiers were often given extra pay for advanced service.[19] Likewise, elders who served well could expect to receive double the financial reward.
       ▷ This does not mean that elders should pursue wealth. Any payment or reward they receive is a reward for excellent service. It is not as though the elder deserves such payment. Rather, such rewards are only for the benefit of those who are willing to humbly serve others.
       ▷ The other danger is to say that since elders are servants, they do not need to be paid. But the text clearly says that elders and ser-

vants receive reward. The key is to have a balanced character that emphasizes service rather than focusing on wealth and reward.
- ▶ This honor extends not only to elders, but also to all who serve. Not all churches can give a salary to those who serve in the church. But the church can still honor these servants through gifts (money or gifts) or by making the ministry of these men and women known to the church. This will then honor their service and encourage the congregation to follow in their example.
- ▶ Servants of God are called to "work hard." Only when one pursues excellence can one be satisfied with one's service.
  - ▷ This means that servants of God should not focus only on money. Those who pursue excellence can feel satisfied. Those who only pursue financial reward can never be satisfied, but in their greed they will always want more.
  - ▷ This also means that God is pleased with one's service. God is pleased with those who work hard for His Kingdom, and will reward them based on how hard and smart they have worked.
- Do not hinder the progress of the Gospel (*1 Timothy 5:18*)
  - ▶ The image of the ox shows the importance of supporting those who work for the Gospel. Oxen and farm animals should be allowed to eat grain. Therefore, elders should be able to receive rewards for what they do. Elders are of greater value than farm animals. Elders work to share the Gospel. Therefore their service is worthy of reward.
  - ▶ One who labors deserves payment. Paul notes his friend Luke, who wrote the books of Luke and Acts in the New Testament. Hard work deserves to be rewarded with payment. Therefore elders should be justly paid and rewarded for their service.
  - ▶ The application here is that elders who are not rewarded may be less able to share the Gospel and serve the community.
    - ▷ Elders often have to work more than one job to support themselves and their families.
    - ▷ Elders who work outside of the church have fewer opportunities to serve inside the church.
    - ▷ Therefore, giving elders just rewards allows them to better serve the church, and everyone benefits from their service.

B. Discipline for drifting elders (*1 Timothy 5:19-25*)
- Be sure evidence of sin is valid (*1 Timothy 5:19-21*)
  - ▶ Not all elders will serve well. Some elders will fall into sin. When this happens, they must be confronted. *Matthew 18:15-20* provides a model for this approach:
    - ▷ *Matthew 18:15-17, "Moreover if your brother sins against you, go and tell him his fault between you and him alone. If he hears you, you have gained your brother. But if he will not hear, take with you one or two more, that 'by the mouth of two or three witnesses every word may be established.' And if he refuses to hear them, tell it to the church. But if he refuses even to hear the church, let him be to you like a heathen and a tax collector."*
    - ▷ Therefore if someone sins:
    - ▷ They must be confronted.

NOTES

- ▷ There must be witnesses.
- ▷ The church must get involved.
- ▷ They may be removed from the church.
  - ▶ Elders who do not respond to this confrontation must be disciplined. This means being disciplined in front of the other elders as well as being disciplined in front of the entire church.
- Distribute discipline as wide as the offense (*1 Timothy 5:20*)
  - ▶ The goal for discipline is to correct the error and allow the elder to be restored to the fellowship of the church. Discipline is therefore not about punishment, but about love.
  - ▶ Not all will respond to this discipline. These men must be treated accordingly. Sin must be dealt with, not ignored or tolerated. This goes for anyone in the church, but elders have a leadership role which makes their sin all the more serious as it can spread to others in the church.

"Fear of the discipline of God... is a healthy thing in a Christian, especially for those in places of leadership. Modern congregations that ignore church discipline do so at the peril of both the offender and themselves."[20]

Question

Are there others you know of that are drifting away from the Gospel? Write down their names below and take a few minutes to pray for them.

How will you confront them in an effort to bring them back into fellowship with the church? Discuss.

Chapter Nine
1 Timothy 6:6-16

Biblical leaders pursue lives of contentment
(*1 Timothy 6:6-16*)

Chapter Overview:

Contentment is being happy with what God has given you. Greed is wanting more.

Serving God does not mean you will become rich. God's servants may or may not be poor. But being poor or having some wealth does not mean they are unhappy. God's leaders find joy in serving, not in how much money they have. Therefore godly leaders do not pursue money or possessions, but instead humbly serve others.

All possessions are temporary. God's promises are eternal. Therefore the attention of God's servants must be given to the eternal things of God, not the riches of earth.

Greed results in immorality. This is often because riches are obtained through sin: stealing, lying, and taking bribes. Greed must be avoided because greed will cause you to commit other sins in order to get more or keep your wealth.

Commentary:

   A. Be content (*1 Timothy 6:6-8*)
      - Contentment is only found in our Lord Jesus (*1 Timothy 6:6-8*)
         ▶ "Contentment" is a word that refers to "great gain." Paul uses this word to describe the attitude of God's servants. God's servants are not to find contentment in money or wealth. They are to find contentment only in Jesus Christ.
         ▶ Contentment in Christ means not finding contentment elsewhere. When we look for contentment elsewhere, we usually are left unhappy.
         ▶ A respected evangelical pastor defines contentment as being free from turmoil within, and satisfied with one's material and financial state, and in possession of a sense of peace, regardless of one's circumstances and feelings.
         ▶ There are many benefits of contentment:
            ▷ Those who are content are able to rest rather than try to find contentment in money or new possessions.
            ▷ Contentment allows us to respect and celebrate other servants without being jealous of them. The danger is to compare ourselves to other people, and feel as though we are not doing enough, not smart enough or are not rich enough. Contentment means being happy for others without feeling envy.
            ▷ Contentment allows us to be grateful. When we are content, we

are able to see where God has blessed us. If we are looking for blessing somewhere else, we may miss an opportunity to thank God for what He has already given.
- ▶ The greatest sign of contentment is godliness. Only a godly man can be content, because contentment can only be found in God.
- Riches are very temporary (*1 Timothy 6:7-8*)
  - ▶ We come into this world with nothing. We leave with nothing. Paul is talking about material possessions. Material things are not eternal. We don't own them when we are born, and we leave them behind when we die.
  - ▶ People work hard to try and get rich and obtain many possessions. But these things are not eternal and have no lasting value. It makes no sense for us to try and obtain many possessions. Instead we must work together for the Gospel, serving others.
  - ▶ The only material possessions man needs are the most basic: food, clothing and shelter. If the Lord takes care of these needs, then there is little reason to pursue more wealth and possessions. These things are God's to give.
  - ▶ *Matthew 6:19-20, "Do not lay up for yourselves treasures on earth, where moth and rust destroy and where thieves break in and steal; but lay up for yourselves treasures in heaven, where neither moth nor rust destroys and where thieves do not break in and steal."*

B. Covetousness always brings disaster (*1 Timothy 6:9-10*)
- It is the root of all types of evil (*1 Timothy 6:9-10*)
  - ▶ To "covet" something means to desire it with all your heart. This is not what God wants. God wants to be the center of our attention. Our love of money and wealth only leads us away from God, toward the false happiness of the world.
  - ▶ Some people make wealth their goal in life. Their purpose is to become rich and powerful. But your purpose cannot be both God's Kingdom and personal wealth. This is why Jesus says that you cannot serve two masters. Those who serve money will learn to hate God. But those who serve God will learn to hate the kind of greed and sin that money can bring.
  - ▶ Paul uses several word pictures to make his point clear.
    - ▷ "Fall into temptation." Falling is something out of our control. When we pursue wealth and money, we lose control and "fall," leading to other sinful behavior, such as lying or stealing to get what we want.
    - ▷ "Snare:" this word refers to a trap. All traps are harmful to those caught in them. When we are trapped by greed, we are unable to serve others in the way God desires.
    - ▷ "Foolish and harmful desires:" these desires trap us and harm us. They harm us spiritually, but our pursuit of wealth can also harm us socially. Those who pursue wealth are selfish, and unable to show God's love to others.
    - ▷ "Plunge:" this word is similar to "fall," though the picture here is to fall into water, to drown. Not only does our greed pull us down, but it drowns us and chokes the spiritual life from us.

- ▷ "Ruin and destruction:" these words refer to the final consequence of greed. Wealth will not bring happiness, but only unhappiness and even punishment.
- ▶ Money is not evil, but loving money leads us into these very types of problems. Greed is a form of idolatry, the act of putting something (in this case money) ahead of God. Only God can satisfy our souls. Therefore we must replace the love of money with the desire to serve God.
- It often leads away from the faith (*1 Timothy 6:10*)
  - ▶ "Longing," in this verse, refers to desire, or to "reach out" for something. In this verse it refers to those who make money their main desire. The ungodly reach out for the wrong things. They look for treasures on earth. The godly reach out for the things of God, such as integrity, honesty and service to others.
  - ▶ To be "pierced with many sorrows" means to feel the damage that greed can bring. Many turn to greed thinking that money can provide happiness. But, instead they find themselves unhappy. In many cases, men have had to steal or lie to obtain their money. In other cases, money is obtained while neglecting to care for the poor or even one's own family. These people quickly find that not only are they unhappy, but they have brought suffering to themselves and their families in pursuit of money and possessions.

C. Paul's personal charge to the man of God (*1 Timothy 6:11-16*)
  - Flee covetousness and lust (*1 Timothy 6:11*)
    - ▶ Believers must be willing to "flee" immoral behavior and greed. This often means running away from situations where these temptations may exist.
    - ▶ Follow godly character qualities (*1 Timothy 6:11*)
      - ▷ Paul lists the qualities as "righteousness, godliness, faith, love, steadfastness, and gentleness."
      - ▷ Notice that greed serves only ourselves. But the qualities Paul lists serve others.
    - ▶ Fight the good fight of faith (*1 Timothy 6:12*)
      - ▷ The "eternal life" and "confession" refer specifically to the content of the Gospel (Christ's death and resurrection) that Timothy and others believed.
      - ▷ To "take hold" of the Gospel means to make it the most important thing. The Gospel should be superior to all discussion of earthly wealth and treasure.
    - ▶ Fulfill your ministry as unto the Lord (*1 Timothy 6:13-14*)
      - ▷ Christ remained faithful in the face of death before Pilate (*1 Timothy 6:13*).
        - ◆ Jesus spoke of "the truth" to Pilate (*John 18:36-38*).
        - ◆ Believers are to follow this example and remain faithful to God's Truth and His Word even in the face of difficulty.
      - ▷ Join the ones who are faithful until He comes again (*1 Timothy 6:14*).
        - ◆ "Keeping the commandment means to remain faithful to God's instructions.

- The coming of Christ gives us hope and joy. To remain faithful does not mean to simply endure difficult times, but to do so knowing that things will one day be perfect when Christ arrives.
- ▶ Remember the mighty King and Lord whom you serve (*1 Timothy 6:15-16*)
    - ▷ Only God, His Word and His people live forever. Therefore only God can be trusted to provide life for others.
    - ▷ Only God deserves glory. No one has seen Him, but we know that His kingdom is far greater than anything that man has on earth. He alone is worthy of our worship.[21]

Question

Do you practice contentment? How will you show and teach contentment in your church?

Chapter Ten
1 Timothy 6:17-19

Godly leaders balance themselves with a proper view of wealth
(*1 Timothy 6:17-19*)

Chapter Overview:

Riches can be dangerous, because they can lead us to believe that we are self-sufficient. We think we can buy whatever we need. But it is God who provides for our needs, not ourselves. Those who trust in their own wealth are in danger of becoming proud rather than the humble servants that God desires.

God's leaders are not to trust in riches, but to focus instead on treasures in heaven. These treasures are stored through earthly service.

One way to keep riches and wealth in perspective is to give away what you do not need. This teaches us to use wealth for the benefit of others. God's people are blessed. Our desire is not to obtain more, but to use that blessing to be a blessing to others. A good relationship with God will provide the leader with knowledge of how to properly spend his money and serve others in God's kingdom.

Commentary:

A. Paul's Challenge to the rich (*1 Timothy 6:17-19*)
- Beware of the self-sufficiency of riches (*1 Timothy 6:18-19*)
  - These verses are about those who are "rich in the present." Paul is making clear that material wealth is only for the present world. Being rich is not always a sign of God's blessing, although it can be at times. The rewards of heaven are more valuable than the riches of this life, even though these rewards are often not seen in this life.
  - Paul gives Timothy a command to "instruct" them. He is to teach them about the way they view wealth.
    - The rich are "not to be conceited." This means that they are not to think highly of themselves or take pride in their wealth. Money often brings pride. Satan can use this to tear down a community of believers.
    - The rich are also "not to hope" in their wealth. Money is unstable. Riches will pass away. The rich should not put their trust in such things, but instead place their faith and trust in God's kingdom.
  - Paul makes clear that riches are uncertain. Material wealth can:
    - Be stolen.
    - Lose its value (through age).
    - Be destroyed.
- Put your security in God (*1 Timothy 6:17*)
  - Unlike material wealth, God cannot change nor can he be destroyed. Believers must put their trust in Him because He is faithful.

- God "richly supplies" us with material blessing. This doesn't mean that God wants us to become rich. It means that God has been generous enough to provide for our basic needs, such as food, clothing and our health. Many people are even able to afford other possessions for their own enjoyment. Greed is not satisfied with these things, and always wants more. Christians are to be satisfied with these things because we understand that these are gifts from God.
- Beware of a wrong use of riches (*1 Timothy 6:18-19*)
    - Use riches for eternity (*1 Timothy 6:18-19*)
        - Christians are to live life God's way. This means working for eternal rewards, not hoping for money and riches while still here on earth. Good works are worthy of praise only if they are free of selfishness.
        - God gives us treasures in heaven. All treasures here on earth will not last. The treasures in heaven show that God loves us and approves of our humility and service.
        - There is an old hymn that says, "Turn your eyes upon Jesus, look full into His wonderful face, and the things of this world will grow strangely dim, in the light of His glory and grace." When Jesus and His Gospel are our greatest treasure, then possessions and money will no longer seem to be of value.
    - Using it properly is laying hold of eternal life (*1 Timothy 6:19*)
        - This verse means that unlike the life on earth that is only temporary, God's promised a future of eternal life.
        - This means that Christians should place their hope not in the temporary riches on earth, but use those riches for the benefit of God's kingdom.
        - The best way to use money is to give it away. This might mean sharing food with a neighbor, or using money to help the poor. When God meets our material needs, then we can use any additional money to be a blessing to others both within the church and outside it.
    - Demonstrate a giving heart (*1 Timothy 6:18*)
        - God shares with us. Therefore those of us who have been richly blessed by Him should follow this example and share with those around us. Giving our money away frees us from the temptation to be greedy, and our resources can be used to bless others.
        - "We will gain contentment when we are grateful for what we own, satisfied with what we earn, and generous to those in need."[22]

B. Paul's challenge to us today
   - Pastors are to be content
     - We must be satisfied with what God has given us. Anything other than contentment is greed. If our basic needs are cared for (food, clothing, and shelter), what else do we really need? What else does God need us to do in order to be happy? Contentment means finding joy with or without the blessing of wealth.
     - Some may find that they have been given the blessing of wealth. Those who are rich can use this blessing to bless others by giving their money to those in need. By doing so, they are showing that

NOTES

  they work for God's eternal Kingdom, and not the possessions of this world.

▶ This is not just advice: it is God's desire: *1 John 3:17, "But whoever has this world's goods, and sees his brother in need, and shuts up his heart from him, how does the love of God abide in him?"*

- Pastors must focus on their relationship with God
  ▶ The only way to know how to use money wisely is through our relationship with God. Only God's Spirit can teach us how to spend money and how to give it away.
  ▶ For this reason, Christians must go to God in prayer and ask Him about how they should spend their money or how they can use it in obedience to Him and His will. This means that Christians are to make it a discipline to study God's Word and spend time in prayer, so that at all times we are able to make wise decisions concerning money.[23]

Questions

Do you desire wealth? How do your desires match with the Bible?

Do you teach a balanced biblical perspective when it comes to wealth and prosperity? Discuss.

THE TIMOTHY INITIATIVE

Section 2: 2 Timothy

Chapter Eleven
Book Outlines & The Charge of Loyalty (2 Timothy 1)

Book Overview:

Chapter 1
Remaining Faithful ....Integrity

Chapter 2
Hard Work ....Excellence in Study

Chapter 3
Preparation for difficult times ....Good Character

Chapter 4
Preaching the Gospel ....Faithfulness

General Outline of 2 Timothy

Theme: Christians must remain faithful to sound doctrine when being persecuted.

1. The charge of loyalty (*Chapter 1*)

    A. Paul's remembrance of Timothy (*2 Timothy 1:1-5*)

    B. Paul's reminder to Timothy (*2 Timothy 1:6-18*)

2. The charge of endurance (*Chapter* 2)

    A. The need to train faithful men (*2 Timothy 2:1-2*)

    B. The importance of enduring hardness (*2 Timothy 2:3-13*)

    C. The necessity for emphasizing the Word (*2 Timothy 2:14-21*)

    D. The role of maturity as a workman (*2 Timothy 2:22-26*)

3. The charge of watchfulness (*Chapter 3*)

    A. Recognize the evil of apostasy (*2 Timothy 3:1-13*)

    B. Recognize the sufficiency of Scripture (*2 Timothy 3:14-17*)

4. The charge of preaching (*Chapter 4*)

    A. The Apostle's urgent commission (*2 Timothy 4:1-5*)

    B. The Apostle's coming departure (*2 Timothy 4:6-8*)

    C. The Apostle's personal desires (*2 Timothy 4:9-13*)

    D. The Apostle's godly dependence (*2 Timothy 14-18*)

    E. The Apostle's salutation and benediction (*2 Timothy 4:19-22*)

Specific Outline of 2 Timothy

1. The charge of loyalty (*Chapter 1*)

    A. Paul's remembrance of Timothy (*2 Timothy 1:1-5*)
   - The greeting (*2 Timothy 1:1-2*)
     - The author – Paul
     - The letter is sent to – Timothy
   - The loving remembrance of his beloved son (*2 Timothy 1:3-5*)
     - Paul's consistent prayers
     - Paul's deep love
     - Timothy's genuine tears
     - Timothy's sincere faith

    B. Paul's reminders to Timothy (*2 Timothy 1:6-18*)
   - Remember to stir up your gift (*2 Timothy 1:6-7*)
     - Timothy has been set apart for shepherding
     - God also provides the power for shepherding
       - Gifts unused are atrophied
       - Fear is not a gift from God
       - Power, love and discipline are of God
   - Remember to endure affliction (*2 Timothy 1:8-12*)
     - Don't be ashamed of the Gospel
     - Don't be ashamed of the Lord or of the apostle Paul
     - Do be mindful of the high calling and power of God
     - Do be mindful of Paul's example
     - Do be mindful of our faithful God in guarding our trust
   - Remember to guard the truth (*2 Timothy 1:13-14*)
     - Maintain true doctrine with faith and love
     - Allow the Holy Spirit to guard the truth
   - Remember to be loyal (*2 Timothy 1:15-18*)
     - Examples of unfaithfulness
       - All in Asia
       - Phygelus and Hermogenes
     - A model of loyalty
       - The household of Onesiphorus
       - The person of Onesiphorus

NOTES

2. The charge of endurance (*Chapter 2*)

   A. The need to train faithful men (*2 Timothy 2:1-2*)
      - Be strong in grace
      - Be mobilizing teachers

   B. The importance of enduring hardness (*2 Timothy 2:3-13*)
      - Like a soldier (*2 Timothy 2:3-4*)
        ▶ He is unencumbered by worldly distractions
        ▶ He is intent on pleasing the Lord
      - Like an athlete (*2 Timothy 2:5*)
        ▶ He is highly disciplined
        ▶ He obeys the rules
      - Like a farmer (*2 Timothy 2:6*)
        ▶ He labors very hard
        ▶ He should receive material support
      - Listen carefully to these words (*2 Timothy 2:7*)
        ▶ Reflection is needed
        ▶ God's understanding will be given
      - Look to Christ's victory over death (*2 Timothy 2:8-13*)
        ▶ Suffering as a partner with Christ
        ▶ Suffering promotes the salvation of the elect
        ▶ Suffering with Christ results in reigning with Him
          ▷ Having died with him we will also live with Him
          ▷ Some will endure and some will deny Him
          ▷ God is faithful

   C. The necessity of emphasizing the Word (*2 Timothy 2:14-20*)
      - Avoid a war of words (*2 Timothy 2:14*)
      - Perfect your handling of the Word (*2 Timothy 2:15*)
        ▶ Study for God's approval
        ▶ Carefully study and teach the Truth
      - Avoid association with false teachers (*2 Timothy 2:16-18*)
        ▶ False teaching is ungodly
        ▶ False teaching hurts people
          ▷ There are many of these wolves in Ephesus
          ▷ Hymenaeus and Philetus sought to devour people
        ▶ False teaching lacks integrity
      - Recognize the certainty and permanence of being in Christ (*2 Timothy 2:19*)
        ▶ God knows who belongs to Him
        ▶ God's children are to abstain from evil
      - Recognize the presence of counterfeits (*2 Timothy 2:20-21*)
        ▶ Some vessels are honorable
        ▶ Some vessels are dishonorable

   D. The role of maturity as a workman (*2 Timothy 2:22-26*)
      - Beware of immoral associations (*2 Timothy 2:22*)
        ▶ Live a Holy life
        ▶ Be useful to Christ

- Be prepared for every good work
- Run from lust and run to righteousness
- Refuse stupid speculations (*2 Timothy 2:23*)
- Teach with patience and reliance on God's inner working (*2 Timothy 2:24-26*)
  - Beware of impatience and arguments
  - Remember only God can change hearts and minds
  - Realize the lost are under Satan's influence

3. The charge of watchfulness (*Chapter 3*)

    A. Recognize the evil of apostasy (*2 Timothy 3:1-13*)
        - The apostasy of the last days (*2 Timothy 3:1-5*)
            - The personal characteristics of false teachers
            - The social characteristics of false teachers
            - The religious characteristics of false teachers
        - The apostasy right now (*2 Timothy 3:6-8*)
            - Passionate motivations
            - False learning
            - Opposed to the Truth
            - Their progress will stop
            - Their foolishness will be obvious to all
        - The expectation of persecution for the Godly (*2 Timothy 3:9-13*)
            - Paul's lifestyle bears witness to this
            - All serious believers will see affliction
            - Evil and deception will increase

    B. Recognize the sufficiency of Scripture (*2 Timothy 3:14-17*)
        - The Word is to be obeyed (*2 Timothy 3:14*)
        - The Word gives wisdom for salvation (*2 Timothy 3:15*)
        - The Word is God-breathed in every part (*2 Timothy 3:16*)
        - The Word is profitable (*2 Timothy 3:16*)
            - For teaching
            - For reproof
            - For correction
            - For training in righteousness
        - The Word perfects the believer for life and service (*2 Timothy 3:17*)
            - God desires a good job
            - God desires proper equipping
            - God desires good service

4. The charge of preaching (*Chapter 4*)

    A. The apostle's urgent commission (*2 Timothy 4:1-5*)
        - The basis of his charge (*2 Timothy 4:1*)
            - God will judge
            - God will appear with His kingdom
        - The essence of his charge (*2 Timothy 4:2-4*)
            - Preach the word

NOTES
- ▸ Preach throughout the year
- ▸ Preach with purpose
- ▸ Preach in light of false doctrine
- The elaboration of his charge (*2 Timothy 4:5*)
  - ▸ Be sober in all things
  - ▸ Persevere in times of difficulty
  - ▸ Work as an evangelist
  - ▸ Complete your ministry

B. The apostle's coming departure (*2 Timothy 4:6-8*)
- His present preparation to depart (*2 Timothy 4:6*)
- His completion of his earthly ministry (*2 Timothy 4:7*)
- His future anticipation of glory (*2 Timothy 4:8*)

C. The apostle's personal desires (*2 Timothy 4:9-13*)
- To see Timothy and Mark (*2 Timothy 4:9-12*)
- To have the cloak, books and papers (*2 Timothy 4:13*)

D. The apostle's godly dependence (*2 Timothy 14-18*)
- Despite Alexander's opposition (*2 Timothy 4:14-15*)
- Despite desertion by friends (*2 Timothy 4:16*)
- Delighting in the Lord (*2 Timothy 4:17-18*)

E. The apostle's salutation and benediction (*2 Timothy 4:19-22*)
- He sends greetings to some special brethren
- He urges Timothy to see him before the winter season
- He requests the Lord's blessing on Timothy

Chapter Overview:

Paul wants Timothy to stand firm during these difficult times. Many in the church were being persecuted, which caused them to leave the church out of fear. Others were leaving the church because of false teachings. Timothy must remain bold and faithful to the Gospel.[24]

This means that he must guard the Gospel. The Gospel is the central focus of the church and ministry. Timothy had shown genuine faith. Paul wanted to encourage him to keep the Gospel — the life, death and resurrection of Jesus — the central teaching in the church.

Paul gives examples of both faithful and unfaithful service. Timothy is to serve faithfully despite the difficulties he faces. Many had turned away from Paul because of the persecutions. But those who remained loyal were highly valued.

Commentary:

A. Paul's remembrance of Timothy (*2 Timothy1: 1-5*)
- The salutation (*2 Timothy1: 1-2*)

- ▶ The author – Paul
  - ▷ Paul describes himself as an "apostle of Christ Jesus."
    - ◆ Paul only sees himself as a servant of God.
    - ◆ To be "an apostle" also means carrying the authority of one sent by God.
  - ▷ "By the will of God" refers to Paul's calling to be an apostle (*Acts 9*). It was God's desire for Paul to be an apostle. God desires for everyone to serve Him.
  - ▷ "The promise" refers to the promise of eternal life through salvation in Jesus Christ. For Paul, service is a natural response to salvation (*Romans 12:1*).
- ▶ The addressee – Timothy
  - ▷ Paul calls Timothy his "beloved son." Though the two men were separated, Paul still had great affection for his fellow servant. Timothy may have been struggling in his leadership position. Paul's letter would have been a great encouragement to him.
  - ▷ Paul begins with a wish for blessing: "grace, mercy and peace." Paul commonly opens his letters by wishing his readers good health and peace. (similar terms are used in *Romans 1:7, 1 Corinthians 1:3, 2 Corinthians 1:2, Ephesians 1:2, Philippians 1:2* and *Colossians 1:2*)
  - ▷ These blessings do not come from Paul, but from God. Though Paul is writing this letter, the blessings he describes are from God alone.
- The loving remembrance of his beloved son (*2 Timothy 1:3-5*)
  - ▶ Paul's consistent prayers (*2 Timothy 1:3*)
    - ▷ Paul is thankful for Timothy. Christians should be thankful for their leaders, and pray for them, as church leaders often face great difficulties.
    - ▷ Paul served with a "clear conscience." All servants of God should model Paul in displaying moral integrity.
    - ▷ Paul's life was filled with prayer. He prayed "night and day." This doesn't mean that there aren't special times that Christians are supposed to pray. Instead, the Christian is meant to use every chance they have to pause and pray to God. Sometimes writing down names of people to pray for on a small paper or card can help you remember to pray for those people.
  - ▶ Paul's deep love (*2 Timothy 1:4*)
    - ▷ Paul speaks of his "longing," his desire to be with Timothy. Paul was in prison at the time of his writing. Yet, he took the time to write to Timothy so that he would remain bold for the Gospel.
    - ▷ Paul says that he wants to see Timothy so he can be "filled with joy." Being together with fellow Christians gives us joy, even during times of struggle and difficulty. This is actually the major theme of the book of Philippians (*Philippians 1:4, 1:25, 2:2, 4:1*).
  - ▶ Timothy's genuine tears (*2 Timothy 1:4*)
    - ▷ Timothy was struggling with leadership in the church. The Roman government was persecuting many people.
      - ◆ This meant that many people were leaving their faith because they were afraid. Timothy was left with a church that was los-

ing its ability to minister to the world because so many were leaving.
- Paul mentions Timothy's "tears." Church leaders can be powerfully affected by struggles in the ministry. One of the reasons to pray for them is so that they will not be worn out by sadness or anger over the struggles they have to deal with.
▷ Timothy was a strong believer, but he needed encouragement to be bold in his faith. Sometimes we look up to leaders and forget that they are human beings. Leaders need prayer and support just as much as anyone, and often face struggles that others do not.
▷ This is a major theme in Scripture.
- *Hebrews tells us: "Consider one another in order to stir up love and good works, not forsaking the assembling of ourselves together, as is the manner of some, but exhorting one another, and so much the more as you see the Day approaching." (Hebrews 10:24-25)*
- We need other believers in our lives to encourage us and challenge us in lives of service.
▶ Timothy's sincere faith (*2 Timothy 1:5*)
▷ Paul writes that he knows about Timothy's "sincere faith."
- The faith of church leaders is easy to take for granted. We should notice the faith of others and tell one another of how much their faith is an encouragement to us.
- Likewise, church leaders should conduct themselves in such a way that their faith can be seen by others. This means living a life of moral character that lets others know that these good works are based on good doctrine.
▷ Timothy's faith is shared by his family.
▷ Families can share their faith from parents to children and even grandchildren.
▷ Entire families can conduct themselves so that others can see their strong faith. This means having a household that displays good character and develops strong faith in the children.
▷ In Deuteronomy, Israel is instructed to teach the children well:
- *"You shall teach them diligently to your children, and shall talk of them when you sit in your house, when you walk by the way, when you lie down, and when you rise up. You shall bind them as a sign on your hand, and they shall be as frontlets between your eyes. You shall write them on the doorposts of your house and on your gates." (Deuteronomy 6:7-9)*
- Likewise, teaching children is an important task that Christians must perform.
▷ Timothy shared the faith of his family. Paul is confident that the same faith that his family had will help Timothy during these hard times.

B. Paul's reminders to Timothy
- Remember to stir up your gift (*2 Timothy 1:6-18*)
▶ Timothy has been set apart for shepherding (*2 Timothy 1:6*)
▷ The reason Paul encourages him is because of Timothy's strong faith. Faith gives us the power to endure times of trouble. Paul

can be confident that Timothy's faith will sustain him during these times of trouble.

- ▷ To "kindle afresh" will remind Timothy of a fire. When a fire starts to die down, it must be fed with small branches so that it can be built up again. Likewise, Timothy must stay strong so that his faith can be built up again. This means using his gifts in ministry without fear.
- ▷ The "gift of God" is Timothy's faith and his God-given ability to be a church leader.
- ▷ The "laying on of hands" refers to a practice where missionaries were commissioned by the other apostles. The apostles would pray for the missionary while laying their hands on him before sending him off. This does not mean that faith comes from this tradition, but it represents the gifts of God being given to the missionary.[25]

▶ God also provides the power for shepherding (*2 Timothy 1:6-7*)
- ▷ Gifts unused are weakened (*2 Timothy 1:6*)
    - ◆ Timothy's gifts must be "kindled afresh." What happens to a fire if you stop feeding it? It goes out. Likewise, there is a danger that when we do not use the gifts God has given us, these gifts will become weak. That means that these gifts (teaching, evangelism, service) will not be able to help the church in the manner that God desires.
    - ◆ A gift cannot be useful if it is hidden. Gifts can become weak when they are not shared with the church, and the church does not receive the benefit of these gifts. It is as if you are working with a group of people and one of them does not want to speak. The group is weaker because not all members are able to work together. Likewise, when a gift is not shared, the entire church suffers because it cannot work together as God desires.
- ▷ Fear is not a gift from God (*2 Timothy 1:7*)
    - ◆ A "spirit" in this verse does not refer to a demon. It refers to a person's attitude.[26]
    - ◆ Timothy's attitude should not be one of fear. The reason so many people were leaving the church was because they were afraid of persecution from the Romans. Paul wanted to make sure that Timothy would not be affected by this same fear.
- ▷ Power, love and discipline are of God (*2 Timothy 1:7*)
    - ◆ God gives his servants the right attitude.
    - ◆ Timothy should not be afraid, but should rely on God's gifts of power, love and discipline.
        - → Power: This word means that Timothy has authority in the church as the leader and is able to proclaim God's message to the culture around him. This doesn't mean power to resist the government, as some in the city were trying to do, but power to serve God.
        - → Love: This word means that Timothy had the ability to serve his church out of love. Some servants of God serve others because they feel as though they have to, not be-

cause they want to. But God gives us love to allow us to serve others out of love for them.
- → Discipline: Timothy needed discipline to fulfill God's mission. Discipline means having the strength to follow God through prayer, study and service, and allowing these to become regular events in his life. As believers, we can have this same gift by making time with God a daily practice.

- Remember to endure affliction (*2 Timothy 1:8-12*)
    - ▶ Don't be ashamed of the Gospel (*2 Timothy 1:8*)
        - ▷ The "testimony of our Lord" refers to the message of the Gospel: the life, death and resurrection of Jesus Christ.
        - ▷ To be "ashamed of the Gospel" means to leave the church because of fear of being persecuted.
        - ▷ Paul writes elsewhere of those who are "ashamed of the Gospel" (*Romans 1:16*). In some places, Paul notes that for some, following the works of the law is a way of avoiding persecution "for the sake of the cross." (*Galatians 6:12*)
    - ▶ Don't be ashamed of the Lord or of the apostle Paul (*2 Timothy 1:8*)
        - ▷ Likewise, believers should not be ashamed because of the sufferings of others. Timothy should not be ashamed of what was happening to Paul.
        - ▷ Paul was a "prisoner" for the Gospel. He had followed God's will, but he was in chains.
            - ◆ This was something that happened to him frequently (*Philippians 1:7, 1:13-17, Colossians 4:3, Philemon 1:10*).
            - ◆ As Christians, our obedience will not always be rewarded in this life. In some cases, obeying God can have painful results, such as prison or even torture and death. It is tempting to walk away from the church when this happens. But Paul warns Timothy not to be ashamed that these things are happening.
    - ▶ Remember the high calling and power of God (*2 Timothy 1:8-10, 11*)
        - ▷ Paul asks that Timothy "join" in his suffering. The ministry is not about glory, but about humble obedience and service. Those who serve God hoping to get rich take for granted the suffering that comes from following Christ.
        - ▷ The suffering Paul is enduring is "for the Gospel." Paul suffers not for reasons of politics or because he was guilty of any crime. Paul suffers for the Gospel.
        - ▷ Suffering for the Gospel is something that can be expected for those who follow God in a world that does not know Him.
        - ▷ The Gospel shows us the "power of God." (*1 Corinthians 1:18*) God's power is revealed in every part of the Gospel.
            - ◆ God "saved us." This is a general term referring to personal salvation, the details are described in the rest of the verse.
            - ◆ God "called us." This means that God has given us a "high calling." God's desire is not only to save us, but also to use us to save others. The gifts we use in church are for God's

purpose in saving others.
- ♦ Salvation and calling are based on God's grace. These are gifts that God gives. They are not earned based on good works. These gifts are given only by the grace of God through Jesus.
- ♦ Salvation and the gift of being called by God are the result of what Christ Jesus has done.
  - → Jesus was part of God's eternal plan. From the very beginning God planned to use Jesus to save sinners. (*John 1:1-18*)
  - → This plan was revealed when Jesus came to earth. Jesus showed God's glory to the world.
  - → The cross and resurrection show that God has defeated death. Those who trust in Him will have eternal life. Therefore, to suffer now is only temporary, for Christians can look forward to eternal life.
- ▷ Paul says (*v. 11*) that it was this message that he preached. All believers are appointed to preach this message, and church leaders like Timothy are given the special task of being an apostle and teacher.
- ▶ Remember Paul's example (*2 Timothy 1:11-12*)
  - ▷ Timothy is likewise to be an "apostle and teacher" like Paul. This means to take the message to unbelievers, as well as teaching good doctrine.
  - ▷ Paul suffers, but he is not ashamed.
    - ♦ The main reason Paul is not ashamed is that he has confidence in God. Paul is encouraged by the fact that he has a relationship with God.
    - ♦ Paul is likewise convinced that he will have eternal life. Paul believes that God will deliver the eternal life He promised, no matter what happens to him in this life on earth.
- ▶ Remember our faithful God in guarding our trust (*2 Timothy 1:12*)
  - ▷ Likewise, Timothy can have confidence in God. God will not lead believers around trouble, but He will lead them through it. Timothy can be confident that God will help him through this difficult time.
  - ▷ Timothy can always count on God's promise. Even death is no longer something to fear, because Timothy can rely on God's promise of eternal life and resurrection.
- • Remember to guard the truth (*2 Timothy 1:13-14*)
  - ▶ Maintain true doctrine with faith and love (*2 Timothy 1:13*)
    - ▷ To "retain" means to hold onto. Unlike those who were leaving the church, Timothy was to hold onto what he believed.
    - ▷ The Gospel Timothy had received had been received from Paul. Unlike the false teachers, Paul had taught the Gospel with "faith and love," qualities that come from Christ Jesus.
  - ▶ Allow the Holy Spirit to guard the truth (*2 Timothy 1:14*)
    - ▷ To "guard" the truth means to defend and protect it. This could mean to guard it from the false teachers who were still in the church, but it most likely means that Timothy is to maintain a lev-

NOTES

el of boldness for the Gospel despite the persecutions and people leaving.
- ▷ The Holy Spirit is the One who does the "guarding." The believer's trust is in God, not his own abilities. Christians can demonstrate this trust by asking God to help them maintain their confidence at all times.
- ▷ The Gospel is called a "treasure." The Gospel is the most valuable gift there is. Money and possessions will fade away, but the Gospel will provide you with eternal life.

- Remember to be loyal (*2 Timothy 1:15-18*)
  - ▶ Examples of the unfaithful (*2 Timothy 1:15*)
    - ▷ All in Asia (*2 Timothy 1:15*)
      - ♦ "You are aware:" Timothy had already received word about those turning away from the faith.
      - ♦ "All in Asia." This could mean a large number or literally everyone, but Paul is making clear that most of the churches that he had reached on his missionary journeys were now leaving the faith in the face of persecution and false teaching.
      - ♦ "Turned away:" this phrase means that they gave up the faith.
        - → When Paul says they turned away from him, he means they have turned away from his message of the Gospel.
        - → Paul and these churches no longer share the same purpose.
    - ▷ Phygelus and Hermogenes (*2 Timothy 1:15*)
      - ♦ Phygelus and Hermogenes are examples of those who turned away.
      - ♦ We don't know who these people are, but the fact that he mentions them means that they were probably once strong Christians.
      - ♦ If even strong Christians are leaving the faith, then it shows how difficult the situation had become.
  - ▶ A model of loyalty (*2 Timothy 1:16-18*)
    - ▷ The household of Onesiphorus (*2 Timothy 1:16*)
      - ♦ Paul asks that God bless the house of Onesiphorus.
      - ♦ We don't know anything about this person other than he was a man from Ephesus who had "refreshed" Paul while he was in prison.
      - ♦ Christians can "refresh" their leaders by bringing them gifts, praying for them, or writing notes of encouragement.
    - ▷ The person of Onesiphorus (*2 Timothy 1:16-18*)
      - ♦ Onesiphorus was not ashamed of Paul's chains.
      - ♦ Onesiphorus was in Rome and found Paul so that he could be an encouragement to him even while in jail.
      - ♦ Therefore, all believers are to follow this example of a man who was not ashamed of Paul's chains, but made the effort to bring encouragement to him.[27]

Questions

Have you seen strong Christians walk away from the faith as a result of persecution? How did that affect your faith? Discuss.

What can you do to encourage others to remain strong in their faith? Write down three things you will do this week in response:

1.

2.

3.

Chapter Twelve
The Charge of Endurance
(2 Timothy 2)

Chapter Overview:

Timothy is again encouraged to be strong and faithful to the Gospel. Timothy had the duty to teach the people in the church, as Paul had instructed him.[28] Paul encouraged him to work hard, using the examples of a soldier, athlete and farmer.

Paul notes that his own life as well as Jesus' life models this level of commitment. Timothy can follow these examples in his own ministry.

Paul describes the ideal servant of God. This servant is one who is not ashamed of the Gospel, but remains faithful in all areas of life; in the church, the home and in his moral behavior.

Churches today face a great deal of difficulty. Those who lead churches must be faithful to the Gospel. This means that they must follow the examples shown in this chapter to ensure that their lives reflect good character and good works that demonstrate the truth of the life-changing power of the Gospel of Jesus Christ.

Commentary:

- A. The need to train faithful men (*2 Timothy 2:1-2*)
  - Be strong in the grace (*2 Timothy 2:1*)
    - ▶ Paul turns from talking about Onesiphorus and those who left the church back to Timothy. Because of the situation the church is in, Timothy must be "strong in the grace."
    - ▶ To be "strong in the grace" means to have a bold commitment to the Gospel. Being strong means not letting fear prevent God's leaders from serving God's mission.
    - ▶ In Hebrews, we learn that there are those who "draw back," (*Hebrews 10:38*), meaning that they turn away from the Gospel.
      - ▷ Persecution will cause people to turn away from the faith.
      - ▷ These people must be encouraged to carry on in the faith.
  - Be leaders who produce leaders (*2 Timothy 2:2*)
    - ▶ God's leaders must produce other leaders (*2 Timothy 2:2*)
      - ▷ "The things you heard from me" refers to the message of the Gospel. Paul often speaks of the Gospel as a message handed down from himself and the other apostles.
      - ▷ Paul tells Timothy to "entrust" this message to "faithful men."
        - ◆ Timothy is to find people in the church who have not left the faith.
        - ◆ These men are to serve as leaders and missionaries in the

church. Paul wants the church to remain strong by building up other leaders who will spread the Gospel.
- ▶ God's leaders will produce teachers (*2 Timothy 2:2*)
  - ▷ These men "will be able to teach others." <u>The purpose of these leaders is therefore not only evangelism, but also to produce other leaders in the church.</u>
  - ▷ Therefore the purpose of these leaders is:
    - ◆ Evangelizing: producing other Christians.
    - ◆ Discipling/Mentoring: producing other leaders and teachers.

Question

This is the passage from which TTI gets is name: The Timothy Initiative. How are you as a student applying this teaching in your life? Discuss.

B. The importance of enduring difficulty (*2 Timothy 2:3-13*)
- • Like a soldier (*2 Timothy 2:3-4*)
  - ▶ He is not bothered by worldly distractions (*2 Timothy 2:4*)
    - ▷ Paul also instructs Timothy to "suffer hardship with me."
      - ◆ Those who leave the church are trying to avoid difficulty. Paul tells Timothy to suffer through it.
      - ◆ Timothy is to suffer "with" Paul. Suffering is not something believers are meant to endure alone. Suffering is more bearable when it is endured together.

Question

How have you suffered for your faith? Have you had someone to suffer with? Will you be willing to suffer with others? Discuss.

- → Solomon taught that *"Though one may be overpowered by another, two can withstand him. And a threefold cord is not quickly broken."* (*Ecclesiastes 4:12*)
- → Therefore, we need to find strong Christians to be in relationship with, so that we may be an encouragement to one another.
  - ▷ Timothy is to suffer with Paul "as a soldier of Jesus Christ." The Christian life is often spoken of as being in spiritual warfare.

NOTES

Christians must therefore be prepared to do battle against the opposing forces of Satan.
- ▶ He is intent on pleasing the Lord (*2 Timothy 2:4*)
  - ▷ A soldier is not distracted by the needs of everyday life. A soldier is focused on his mission.
  - ▷ A soldier desires to complete his mission because he wants to please the ones who gave the commands.
  - ▷ Christian soldiers are to serve God Who calls them into His service. Christians should not be distracted by earthly needs and desires, but be faithful in their commitment to God's mission and Kingdom.
- Like an athlete (*2 Timothy 2:5*)
  - ▶ He is highly disciplined (*2 Timothy 2:5*)
    - ▷ To be a good athlete means that you train well. This takes lots of time to prepare for the race or event. Athletes have to be disciplined and train every day to be able to perform well.
    - ▷ Likewise, Christians are to be disciplined in their spiritual lives. Bible study, prayer and service help Christians prepare for times of difficulty when spiritual endurance is needed.
  - ▶ He obeys the rules (*2 Timothy 2:5*)
    - ▷ Athletes have to obey the rules. Cheating will cause the athlete to lose the race, because these events have judges in them.
    - ▷ Likewise, Christians must obey the rules. Their lives must display moral character and integrity. Their good works show unbelievers the value of what they believe.
- Like a farmer (*2 Timothy 2:6*)
  - ▶ He labors very hard (*2 Timothy 2:6*)
    - ▷ Farmers work very hard. Farmers have to be disciplined in order to plant and harvest their crops.
    - ▷ Likewise, Christians are to be hardworking. A Christian cannot be lazy. A Christian is to work hard and serve others with excellence.
  - ▶ He should receive material support (*2 Timothy 2:6*)
    - ▷ The farmer will also receive "his share" at the time of harvest.
    - ▷ Likewise, Christian leaders deserve payment for their service. This does not mean that Christian leaders should be greedy, but that their service is rewarded justly based on the excellence of their service.

Question

What do you do if the people in your new house church/fellowship are not able to pay you? Are you willing to stay with them even in difficult times? Discuss.

- Listen carefully to these words (*2 Timothy 2:7*)
  - Reflection is needed (*2 Timothy 2:7*)
    - Paul tells Timothy to "consider" these things. To "consider" means to reflect or think deeply.
    - Timothy must think deeply about what Paul has shared. Christians are meant to be deep thinkers. This doesn't mean that Christians must be smart, but it does mean that Christians take the time to think about what God has told them through His Word.
  - God's understanding will be given (*2 Timothy 2:7*)
    - Sometimes God's Word is hard to understand. Paul tells Timothy that God will give him understanding.
    - Christians can rely on God to help them understand His Word.
      - This still means that they must study hard. But they can rely on God to help them understand what they are studying.
      - Christians can begin their times of study by asking God to help them understand what they read.
- Look to Christ's victory over death (*2 Timothy 2:8-13*)
  - Suffering as a partner with Christ (*2 Timothy 2:8-9*)
    - Timothy is told to "remember Jesus Christ."
      - The reason Christians can endure hardship is because they remember that it was God's plan for Christ to suffer, die and to rise again.
      - Christ's victory over death means that Christians suffer in this life only. Christians may endure suffering, confident in the eternal life promised to them through Jesus.
    - Paul suffers as Christ had suffered. Christ had suffered on the cross, and now Paul suffers in a prison cell. Paul endures this suffering for the sake of the Gospel, because it is this message that had caused him to be imprisoned.
    - God's Word cannot be stopped!
      - Though Paul was put in prison, his message was still being spread.
      - Persecution does not stop the Gospel. In fact, those who endure persecution are often more willing to spread the Gospel than ever before. God can use even the very worst situations for His eternal purpose and for His glory.
  - Suffering promotes the salvation of those who are chosen (*2 Timothy 2:10*)
    - Paul also endures hardship for the sake of other believers. The "chosen" in this verse refers to God's eternal plan of salvation. Those who trust in Christ can find comfort in knowing that God chose them "before the foundation of the world."
    - Those who are chosen can receive salvation. This means that God chooses believers to receive the gift of salvation through Jesus Christ, and the eternal rewards of Heaven.
  - Suffering with Christ results in reigning with Him (*2 Timothy 2:11-13*)
    - Having died with him we will also live with Him (*2 Timothy 2:11*)
      - Christians are united with Jesus in His death and resurrection (*Romans 6:8*). When we place our faith in Christ, we die to our "old self" and are forgiven our sins.

- But since Jesus was raised from the dead, we are also raised with Him. Because He lives, we have the hope in the promise of eternal life in the presence of the Father.
  ▷ Some will endure and some will deny Him (*2 Timothy 2:12*)
    - Some will endure, meaning that some will remain faithful to the Gospel. These people will receive the rewards for their faithfulness.
    - Others will deny God. These are the people who leave the church out of the fear of persecution. Paul says that God will deny these people. They are not denied their justification or salvation but they are denied some of their eternal reward. There is loss of eternal reward.
  ▷ God is faithful (*2 Timothy 2:13*)
    - Paul comforts Timothy in saying that even if we are "faithless," God remains "faithful." To be "faithless" means to live for something other than Jesus and the Gospel. But Jesus died even for the faithless. Some reward may be gone for the faithless but Jesus cannot deny Himself, therefore the believer is still justified.
    - Since God is faithful, we can trust in Him to give us the faith to believe in Him as well as the strength to endure persecution and hardships.
    - God is faithful because "He cannot deny Himself." It is in God's nature to be faithful. God's faithfulness is a part of His character and He will not change or leave us during times of difficulty. True children of God cannot become something other than children, even when disobedient or weak. Christ's faithfulness to Christians is not based on performance or faithfulness.[29]

C. The obligation to call attention to the Word (*2 Timothy 2:14-20*)
  - Avoid a war of words (*2 Timothy 2:14*)
    ▶ Timothy is told to "remind them" of what Paul has said concerning the Gospel.
      ▷ Timothy is to constantly tell this church about the Gospel of Jesus Christ.
      ▷ The Gospel is not just something we proclaim for evangelism, but is a message that the church needs to hear all the time, as it can instruct us for Christian living.
    ▶ Timothy is also to tell this church to avoid arguments. This means to not waste time arguing about matters other than the Gospel. The Gospel is so important that it is foolish to waste time arguing about things.
    ▶ Arguments lead to ruin.
      ▷ The Gospel leads to salvation and to good works. Arguing over human doctrines will not produce salvation or good works.
      ▷ Arguing only hurts other people and causes more conflict. Believers are to avoid arguments that cause others to walk away from the church.
  - Perfect your handling of the Word (*2 Timothy 2:15*)

- ▶ Study for God's approval (*2 Timothy 2:15*)
  - ▷ Paul tells Timothy to "be diligent." Paul encourages hard work. To "be diligent" means to work hard. In this verse, it means to work hard to study God's word and learn about Him.
  - ▷ The purpose of this hard work was so that Timothy could "present himself as one approved." "Approved" means to be "tested." It was used to refer to testing metals, to see if there were any imperfections. Paul is saying that one who is "approved" in God's eyes is one who is able to use the Bible well.
- ▶ Carefully study and teach the Truth (*2 Timothy 2:15*)
  - ▷ "Rightly dividing the word of truth" means to be able to correctly study and teach God's word. The Greek word means "to cut straight." Cutting along a straight line takes a steady hand and much concentration. Likewise, a correct interpretation of God's Word takes patience, concentration and discipline.
    - ◆ This often takes years of training and study, but is very rewarding to those who have the discipline.
    - ◆ It may be that the false teachings that Paul writes about are the result of lazy students. They could not teach God's truth accurately, so they taught words of human wisdom instead. God's leaders are called to be good students.
  - ▷ Those who "rightly divide" God's Word are not only able to interpret what it says, but to apply it in their lives. This is why James says that believers are meant to be "doers" of the Word, not just those who hear God's Word and do not obey it (*James 1:22-23*). Christian leaders must be men of the Word, both in their ability to explain it as well as their desire to live by it.
- • Avoid association with false teachers (*2 Timothy 2:16-18*)
  - ▶ False teaching is ungodly (*2 Timothy 2:16*)
    - ▷ Timothy is to avoid "worldly and empty chatter." This refers to the human words that are used in false teaching. The false teachers were probably Jewish in origin, but had learned to borrow ideas from other cultures, writers and religions. The result was a system of ideas that were very different from the Gospel that Paul had been preaching. Timothy must avoid this type of teaching at all costs.
    - ▷ One of the reasons to avoid this teaching is that false teaching leads to more ungodliness. False teaching is like a disease that spreads in the body of the church. The Gospel brings life and good works. False teaching leads to immorality.
  - ▶ False teaching hurts people (*2 Timothy 2:17*)
    - ▷ There are many of these wolves in Ephesus (*2 Timothy 2:17*)
      - ◆ Paul compares the false teaching to "gangrene." Gangrene is a sickness that damages parts of the body. Likewise, false teachings bring damage to the body of Christ, the church.[30]
      - ◆ Words can be harmful. Satan knows this. False teaching can be even more damaging to the church than outside persecution. Persecution can be endured, but false teaching will cause believers to fall into error concerning the Gospel they believe. The result is that they no longer have any power to

take the Gospel to the world as God desires.
- ▷ Hymenaeus and Philetus sought to devour people (*2 Timothy 2:17-18*)
  - ◆ We don't know much about Hymenaeus and Philetus except what Paul shares here. Hymenaeus was mentioned in *1 Timothy*, so we know that these false teachings were an ongoing problem.
  - ◆ These false teachers said that the resurrection had already taken place. This was a teaching that came from "Gnosticism." These people taught that the resurrection was only "spiritual," and there was no actual resurrection of the body. The body didn't matter. In the Corinthian church, this led to many problems. These were strange ideas that Timothy was told to avoid.
  - ◆ The reason these doctrines were so dangerous was because Paul says that some had already had their faith challenged by these strange ideas. False doctrine must be avoided in order to protect the faith of people in the church and keep them from falling into ungodliness.
- ▶ False teaching lacks integrity (*2 Timothy 2:18*)
  - ▷ Paul says that these men had "gone astray." This means that they may have started out understanding some parts of the Gospel, but had changed it based on this new teaching.
  - ▷ To have integrity means to accept the Gospel as it has been given.
    - ◆ Sometimes it is tempting to try and add to the Gospel in order to make it sound better. For example, some may try and say that belief in God will result in great wealth. This is a message that sounds very good and many will like. But it is not true.
    - ◆ Others seek to add to the Gospel saying that it is too simple and must be more complex. Others seek to make the Gospel full of spiritual mysteries to the point that it cannot be understood by its clear meaning. These also are bad lies.
    - ◆ Faithful servants of God must avoid such teaching and remain faithful to the message that has been delivered through Paul and the apostles.
- • Recognize the certainty and stability of being in Christ (*2 Timothy 2:19*)
  - ▶ God knows who belongs to Him (*2 Timothy 2:19*)
    - ▷ "The firm foundation of God stands." God's truth does not change with the culture. God's Truth is the same today, yesterday and forever.
    - ▷ God knows who are His. Those who reject God's Truth and God's Word do not belong to Him.
    - ▷ At the same time, God knows who are His. This does not mean that Christians are always able to tell who belongs to God. It may be that some false teachers are struggling with doubt and that God can still use this situation to pull them back to Him. Christians are to respond by avoiding these teachings and discipline those who follow them, with the final goal of restoring these teachers to fellowship with God and His church.
  - ▶ God's children are to avoid immorality (*2 Timothy 2:19*)

- ▷ God's children are also characterized by their works. God's children are to avoid immoral behavior.
- ▷ Scripture makes clear that good doctrine leads to good fruit. The immoral actions of these false teachers only reveal the false doctrines that they teach.
- ▷ Those who call God their Father should love the things that God loves. Therefore Christians are to love God's church and love God's holy character. Their actions should reflect their love for this purity.

- Recognize the presence of counterfeits (*2 Timothy 2:20*)
  - ▶ Some vessels are honorable (*2 Timothy 2:20*)
    - ▷ In a house there are gold and silver vessels, or bowls. Gold and silver were expensive materials. These household items were therefore very high quality. They are also long lasting and hard to break.
    - ▷ These high-quality items represent believers who are faithful and remain devoted to God's Truth. And like the metal dishes, this devotion also makes them long lasting, rather than those who follow false teachings.
  - ▶ Some vessels are dishonorable (*2 Timothy 2:20*)
    - ▷ Other vessels are made of wood and clay. These were cheaper quality materials and were easier to break.[31]
    - ▷ Those who follow false teachings are like these lesser quality dishes. They are less likely to withstand hardship, unlike the gold and silver dishes. Those led astray by false teachings will find their lives less stable then those who remain faithful to God's Truth.

D. The role of maturity as a workman (*2 Timothy 2:21-26*)
  - Beware of immoral associations (*2 Timothy 2:21, 22*)
    - ▶ Live a Holy life (*2 Timothy 2:21*)
      - ▷ To "cleanse" yourself from these vessels means to follow their teaching and their standards of conduct.
      - ▷ To be "sanctified" means to be set apart for God's Holy purposes. Those who remain faithful will find purpose in God's kingdom.
        - ✦ In John's Gospel, Jesus prays that God would "sanctify" His disciples "by your truth, your word is truth." (*John 17:17*)
        - ✦ Likewise, Christians are to be set apart through obedience to Scripture.
    - ▶ Be useful to Christ (*2 Timothy 2:21*)
      - ▷ Christ is described as the "Master." No matter how spiritually mature a believer is, Christ has total authority over him.
      - ▷ To be "useful" to Christ means to be able to participate in Christ's mission, to take the Gospel to every part of the earth.
    - ▶ Be prepared for every good work (*2 Timothy 2:21*)
      - ▷ "Every good work" is a general term. It refers to all behavior that conforms to God's Holy character.
      - ▷ Good doctrine is the source for this ability. Those who practice false doctrine are not able to do good works, because their doctrine does not teach this. Good doctrine leads us to righteous character and good works.

- Run from lust and run to righteousness (*2 Timothy 2:22*)
  - This verse describes how a believer can be a vessel used for God's righteous purpose.
  - Run from lust. The image here is of running away, the way you might run away from a fight. Sin is a fight you will always lose. Therefore, Christians should avoid all temptations.
  - Run to righteousness. The Christian life is not just about avoiding sin, but about pursuing good works. Christians should pursue God's righteous character through good works that display "faith, love and peace."
  - These traits are to be found in the presence of other sincere believers. The Christian is to pursue God's righteousness "with those who call on the Lord from a pure heart." This means that other believers can be an encouragement to pursue good works. Sin always pushes us away from one another. Love and good works draw us together. When we are alone, we are in the most danger of falling into sin.
  - This text here also affirms the need for Timothy and for us today to stay pure in relationships with the opposite sex. God wants us to avoid foolish and ignorant speculations that lead to quarrels... and to pursue righteousness, faith and love with those who call on the Lord with a pure heart. There is no better text in all of Scripture regarding what a relationship should look like with a man and a woman who are spending time together and getting to know one another.
- Refuse stupid speculations (*2 Timothy 2:23*)
  - Being useful to God also means that Timothy must avoid the "foolish" and "ignorant" speculations of the false teachers. The words that Paul uses mean that these ideas are not based on knowledge. They are just stupid human ideas that are being taught instead of God's Truth.
  - These speculations are to be avoided because they divide the church body by creating fights and arguments.
    - The word "quarrel" is a word that in the first century had to do with actual military combat.[32]
    - Good doctrine leads to unity in the body of Christ. These other ideas only create fights and division.
- Teach with patience and reliance on God's inner working (*2 Timothy 2:24-26*)
  - Beware of impatience and arguments (*2 Timothy 2:24-25*)
    - Because of all this division, impatience and arguments are meant to be avoided. Timothy, and all leaders, are to avoid being the type of leader who generates fights and arguments.
    - Instead of being "quarrelsome," God's leaders are to possess positive qualities.
      - "Kind to all" means that unlike the false teachers, who were likely to argue with those who disagreed, God's servants are called to show kindness to everyone. This kindness shows the goodness of God's Truth.
      - They must be "able to teach," because it is important for

God's Truth to be passed on to others so that all may share in the joy of salvation through Christ's Gospel.
- "Patient when wronged" means that if someone harms them or insults them, they do not seek revenge against the person who wronged them, but are able to forgive.
- Correct error "with gentleness." The false teachers used arguments and fights to try and teach their false doctrine. Good doctrine must be taught with good works and humility. Humility renders evil useless.

▶ Remember only God can change hearts and minds (*2 Timothy 2:25*)
  ▷ The response of church leaders to rival doctrine is with the final goal that the false teachers repent and return to "the knowledge of the truth."
  ▷ It is only God who can do this. Only God can grant understanding to His children.
    - This is the reason that Timothy is told to be patient and gentle. If only God can change someone's heart and mind, then foolish arguments are of no use.
    - Only gentleness and kindness can allow the false teachers to become open to God who will lead them to His truth.

▶ Realize the lost are under Satan's influence (*2 Timothy 2:26*)
  ▷ The false teachers and the lost are trapped by the devil. This is the reason for such deception.
    - The words "snare" and "captive" show that they are trapped. They are helpless, because they are under Satan's influence.
    - Therefore, church leaders must be gentle, because rather than being angry with these men, we must feel sorry for them, as they are trapped and caught.
    - This does not mean that these men are not responsible for their actions. We may feel sorry for them, but these men are still responsible for their false teaching and immoral behavior.
  ▷ The hope of church leaders is that these men might escape from this harmful influence. Only by being freed from Satan's influence can these men find hope in Jesus Christ and see the moment power of the Holy Spirit.[33]

Chapter Thirteen
The Charge of Watchfulness
(2 Timothy 3)

Chapter Overview:

Timothy is instructed to be watchful. Paul is referring to the "last days." The last days are the time that Paul wrote the letter until the day that Christ returns. This means that we are also living in the last days.

The last days will be marked by more and more false teachers and false teachings. Paul describes the faithless characteristics of these false teachers, comparing them to characters in the Old Testament who refused to listen to Moses.

Paul goes on to describe the need for faithful moral conduct in the last days. This means that God's servants must be faithful in correctly teaching the Word, and faithful in applying it to their lives and proclaiming the Gospel to others.

The church will always face difficulty, until the day that Christ comes back. God's servants must be prepared for these difficulties by modeling their lives after Christ, and by being disciplined in learning Scripture and teaching others about Jesus.

Commentary:

- A. Recognize the evil of apostasy (*2 Timothy 3:1-13*)
  - The apostasy of the last days (*2 Timothy 3:1-5*)
    - ▶ The personal characteristics of false teachers (*2 Timothy 3:1-2*)
      - ▷ "Last days:" refers to the whole time from the time the letter was written until the return of Christ.
      - ▷ "Difficult times:" the closer we get to the return of Christ, the more we can expect false teachers to arise.
      - ▷ False teachers are defined by these characteristics:
        - ◆ "Lovers of self:" false teachers are self-centered, not loving others.
        - ◆ "Lovers of money:" they pursue money, not the truth.
        - ◆ "Revilers:" they have no respect for God or His Truth.
        - ◆ "Disobedient to parents:" they do not respect their parents.
        - ◆ "Ungrateful:" greedy people cannot be grateful for what they have.
        - ◆ "Unholy:" they practice immorality.
        - ◆ "Unloving:" they lack any natural love whatsoever.
        - ◆ "Irreconcilable:" they do not forgive others or fix broken relationships.
        - ◆ "Malicious gossips:" they speak poorly of others, often saying things that aren't true.

- "Without self-control:" they cannot control their need for pleasure.
- "Brutal:" they are unkind and hurt others with their words.
- "Haters of Good:" their lives are opposed to the character of God.
- "Treacherous:" they are not honest with others and will betray one another.
- "Reckless:" they are not patient or kind, but ignore all of God's commands.
- "Lovers of pleasure rather than lovers of God:" they seek pleasure in earthly things rather than God's Kingdom.
- "A form of Godliness:" they may seem to be religious. But they do not believe the Gospel or live a fruitful life.

- The apostasy right now (*2 Timothy 3:6-9*)
  - Passionate motivations (*2 Timothy 3:6*)
    - The false teachers include those who seek out women.
    - Women during these days in Ephesus were less educated ("gullible women") and were more likely to embrace these false teachings.
    - This does not mean that these women were weaker than men, just more easily persuaded by false teachers. They did not have as much training as men at this time in Ephesus.
  - False learning (*2 Timothy 3:7*)
    - These false teachers look like good students. They are always learning.
    - The learning these teachers enjoy does not lead them to the Truth. They read many books, but not the Bible.
    - When Paul was in Athens, there were many who loved learning new ideas, but few who accepted the truth of the Gospel of Jesus Christ (*Acts 17:21, 32*).
  - Opposed to the Truth (*2 Timothy 3:8*)
    - Jannes and Jambres are not mentioned in the Bible.
      - Jews thought that these were two of the magicians who went against Moses (*Exodus 7:11*).
      - These men opposed Moses in favor of their own lies.
    - Likewise, false teachers embrace their own ideas rather than the Gospel.
  - Their progress will stop (*2 Timothy 3:9*)
    - They will not be able to spread their ideas. If God is not in it, then no idea can spread very far.
    - Only the Gospel has the power to be spread to every nation.
  - Their foolishness will be obvious to all (*2 Timothy 3:9*)
    - False teachers are prideful and value the respect of others.
    - But others will come to understand the foolishness of these false teachings. These false teachers will become fools in the eyes of those they try and impress.
- The expectation of persecution for the godly (*2 Timothy 3:10-13*)
  - Paul's lifestyle bears witness to this (*2 Timothy 3:10-11*)
    - Timothy followed in Paul's example:
      - Teaching

NOTES

- Conduct
- Purpose
- Faith
- Patience
- Love
- Perseverance
  ▷ Paul also experienced persecution
    - At Antioch (*Acts 13:14, 51*)
    - At Iconium (*Acts 14:1-7*)
    - At Lystra (*Acts 14:8-23*)
▶ All serious believers will see hardship (*2 Timothy 3:12*)
  ▷ Suffering is not something to be avoided.
  ▷ Paul says that persecution will happen to serious believers.
    - This means that those who avoid suffering might not be a serious believer.
    - If you avoid suffering, it may mean you are ashamed of the Gospel.
▶ Evil and deception will increase (*2 Timothy 3:13*)
  ▷ There will be more and more false teachers in the future.
  ▷ False teachers deceive others and are themselves deceived.
    - False teachings make men foolish.
    - These foolish men become teachers and spread this false teaching to others.

B. Recognize the sufficiency of Scripture (*2 Timothy 3:14-17*)
  - The Word is to be obeyed (*2 Timothy 3:14*)
    ▶ "The things you have learned" refer to both:
      ▷ Scripture.
      ▷ The Gospel received from Paul.
    ▶ Timothy is instructed to obey these teachings.
      ▷ Timothy had learned these teachings and become certain of them.
      ▷ Timothy knows the source of these teachings: God and the Holy Spirit.
  - The Word gives wisdom for salvation (*2 Timothy 3:15*)
    ▶ Timothy had known these Scriptures from childhood.
      ▷ Young people need good teaching.
      ▷ Solomon writes: *"Train up a child in the way he should go, And when he is old he will not depart from it."* (*Proverbs 22:6*)
        - This is not a guarantee that children will develop into mature, Christian adults. It is an saying that is the normal way that God works in His people.
        - Parents must remain faithful in teaching their children the ways of the Lord.
    ▶ The Bible leads to salvation, because the Bible contains the Gospel.
  - The Word of God is God-breathed in every part (*2 Timothy 3:16*)
    ▶ The Bible is "God-breathed." It is often referred to as "inspired."
      ▷ The word means "to blow," like a sail on a sailing ship being blown by the wind, which moves the boat forward.
      ▷ Likewise, the writers of the Bible wrote, but the Holy Spirit guided their thoughts.

- This does not mean God told them what to say as in a mechanical dictation, or in some stiff fashion.
- The Bible's authors wrote the Bible in their own cultures with their own vocabulary.
- But God was in their hearts, making sure the final product was what He wanted to say: *2 Peter 1:21, "for prophecy never came by the will of man, but holy men of God spoke as they were moved by the Holy Spirit."*
  ▷ This included the Old Testament, but *2 Peter 1:20-21* refers to Paul's writings as part of Scripture: *2 Peter 3:16, "as also in all his epistles, speaking in them of these things, in which are some things hard to understand, which untaught and unstable people twist to their own destruction, as they do also the rest of the Scriptures."*
  ▷ The "rest of Scripture" means that Paul's letters were a part of the Bible from the very beginning. The Holy Spirit was writing through Paul and other Biblical authors, using the writer's mind, heart, spirit and also providing supernatural leadership and empowerment in the process.
- The word is profitable (*2 Timothy 3:16*)
  ▶ For teaching: to instruct people on God's Truth.
  ▶ For reproof: this word means to have a strong commitment to doctrine.
  ▶ For correction: to make something right.
  ▶ For training in righteousness: to develop a holy and moral character.
- The Word perfects the believer for life and service (*2 Timothy 3:17*)
  ▶ God desires a good job
    ▷ The purpose of Scripture is so that the Christian may be complete.
      - "Complete" means to be able to do something, or to be capable.
        → Christian leaders are meant to be able to do God's will and perform His tasks well.
        → Scripture provides the manual for how to do this. By being good students of Scripture, Christians can be confident that they will be capable of living lives of good works.
      - God makes His servants complete: *Hebrews 13:20-21* tells us that God will *"make you complete in every good work to do His will, working in you what is well pleasing in His sight."*
        → God wants to equip His servants so that they may serve Him better than ever before.
        → God is pleased when His servants serve Him well. Christian leaders can be confident that God approves of their service.
    ▷ Being "complete" means being capable of doing "every good work."
      - This means that servants of God do good works. Their character reveals their beliefs.
      - This also means that servants of God are capable of performing the work of the ministry, whether it is teaching, serving or hospitality.

NOTES

NOTES

- God desires proper equipping
  - "Fully equipped" means to be well prepared.
  - Servants of God receive their preparation from God and His Word.
- God desires good service
  - "Every good work" refers to all good works of Christian living.
  - Paul is saying that what you believe can be seen by others based on the works you do.
    - This is why James says that "faith without works is dead."
    - Works do not bring salvation, but works show others the content of your belief. Good works in Jesus Christ reveal the reality and purity of our walks with God. We live in these good works through the power of the Holy Spirit. He is our Power and our Source for living in the Lord and for His Kingdom.[34]

Question

How can you know that the Bible is God's word? What do you tell others when they ask you? Discuss.

Chapter Fourteen
The Charge of Preaching
(2 Timothy 4)

Chapter Overview:

Timothy is given the clear instruction to preach the Gospel. Christian leaders must make this the central work of the ministry. This also means being prepared at all times to minister to others and to teach others God's Truth.

The Gospel is not always popular. Many people will turn away from the Gospel and follow teachings that are untrue, but sound good. Ministers of the Gospel must be aware of this and prepared to face this rejection.

Paul is nearing the end of his life, and wishes for the comforts of friendship and God's Word. We must remember to serve others by being friends to them and to minister to them using God's Word.

Commentary:

A. The apostle's urgent commission (*2 Timothy 4:1-5*)
- The basis of his charge (*2 Timothy 4:1*)
  - ▶ God will judge
    - ▷ These verses are Paul's final instructions to Timothy. He wants his words to have a great deal of force.
      - ◆ To "charge" means to encourage strongly.
      - ◆ Paul wants Timothy to understand how serious these words are.
    - ▷ Jesus' presence is the basis for these instructions. Christ's character is what motivates God's servants for ministry.
      - ◆ Jesus is the judge of all, living and dead.
      - ◆ His appearing on earth reveals the truth of the Gospel.
      - ◆ His Kingdom refers to His second coming.
  - ▶ God will appear with His kingdom
    - ▷ The reality of God's coming Kingdom motivates God's servants for work here and now.
    - ▷ In the first century, they believed God was coming back very soon. Therefore they wanted to work fast.
      - ◆ We do not know when Jesus is returning (*Acts 1:7-8*). Therefore we should work as if He might return at any moment.
- The essence of his charge (*2 Timothy 4:2-4*)
  - ▶ Preach the Word (*2 Timothy 4:2*)
    - ▷ "The Word" here means the Gospel and all God's Truth in Scripture.
    - ▷ Preaching requires discipline and perseverance.

- Preach throughout the year (*2 Timothy 4:2*)
  - "In season and out of season" refers to year-round ministry.
  - The preaching of the Gospel should be the focus of any Christian ministry.
  - Problems such as false teachings become worse when God's servants do not make the Gospel their central focus.
- Preach with purpose (*2 Timothy 4:2*)
  - Reprove: make the beliefs of the church stronger
  - Rebuke: correct those who are in sin or believe false doctrine.
  - Exhort: encourage the church to stand strong in their faith.
- Preach in light of false doctrine (*2 Timothy 4:3-4*)
  - Sound doctrine is not always popular.
    - People will not always want to hear the Gospel.
      - The Gospel speaks of things that are not popular such as sin and judgment.
      - These things are true and can save people. Therefore it must be preached.
    - They will want to hear teaching that makes them feel good. "Itching ears" means that they want teaching that makes them happy, rather than teaching that is true.
  - False teachers will rise
    - In the future, these teachers will become more common.
    - Church leaders are chosen based on character. These teachers are based on how popular they are among the people.
  - People will turn away from the Gospel.
    - "Myths" refer to teachings that sound better but are not true.
    - Paul may have been concerned that Timothy was in danger of turning away. This section is to encourage him to remain faithful to the Gospel.

- The explanation of his charge (*2 Timothy 4:5*)
  - Be sober in all things: this means to be "watchful" or to be alert. We need to be aware of what's going on and how it might affect the ministry.
  - Persevere in times of difficulty: this means not to give up or turn away as others have.
  - Work as an evangelist: this means to preach the Gospel to people and see others led to Christ.
  - Complete your ministry: this means to keep working for the sake of the Gospel, to do what God has called His servants to do.

B. The apostle's coming departure (*2 Timothy 4:6-8*)
- His present preparation to depart (*2 Timothy 4:6*)
  - Paul is being "poured out like a drink offering."
    - A "drink offering" was an offering performed by pouring wine on the ground or altar (*Numbers 28:11-31*).[35]
    - Likewise, Paul was being "poured out," that is, used in service to God.
  - Paul seemed to know that he was about to die. The "time of my departure" shows that Paul was preparing to pass from this life into heaven.

NOTES

- His completion of his earthly ministry (*2 Timothy 4:7*)
  - ▶ Paul says that he has done all that he was called to do, and served well.
  - ▶ Paul describes his faith and service as a race.
    - ▷ This type of language was common in the New Testament.[36]
    - ▷ Paul writes elsewhere of "pressing onward to the prize," (*Philippians 3:14*) and encourages his readers to press onward as well (*1 Corinthians 9:24-25*).
- His future anticipation of glory (*2 Timothy 4:8*)
  - ▶ Paul is confident that he will receive a reward for service.
    - ▷ A "crown of righteousness" is a reward to those who serve God faithfully on earth.
    - ▷ Jesus promises rewards for those who endure persecution and difficulty (*Matthew 5:10-12*).
  - ▶ God gives these rewards because He is the "righteous judge." God rewards those who are faithful to Him.
  - ▶ All Christians who persevere and remain faithful may expect to receive a reward for their faithful service.
    - ▷ "Those who have loved His appearing" refers to those who hope for the Lord's return (*Titus 2:11-15; 1 John 2:28*).
    - ▷ Believers are to count on Christ not only in this life, but the next. This is why Paul tells his readers to live as "citizens of heaven" (*Philippians 3:20*).

C. The apostle's personal desires (*2 Timothy 4:9-13*)
  - To see Timothy and Mark (*2 Timothy 4:9-12*)
    - ▶ At the end of his life, Paul values his friends.
      - ▷ Luke is with Paul
      - ▷ Demas is Paul's coworker (*Colossians 4:14, Philemon 24*). Apparently he was not faithful to the Gospel and left Paul. He deserted the faith.
      - ▷ Paul wants Timothy to come visit
      - ▷ Paul wants Timothy to bring Mark
        - ✦ Mark had not always been faithful. He deserted Paul in Pamphylia. Paul did not want to take Mark along on his second missionary journey, which led to a disagreement with Barnabas (*Acts 15:36-40*).
        - ✦ Paul mentions here that Mark is "useful," which shows that Mark has been restored as a fellow disciple. The Holy Spirit used Barnabas to fulfill his calling in bring John Mark back to Jesus.
        - ✦ All Christians can be useful to God, no matter what their past behavior has been. Church leaders must be willing to give second chances to servants of God.
    - ▶ Christians must find value in close friendships, even more important during times of great difficulty and hardship.
  - To have the cloak, books and papers (*2 Timothy 4:13*)
    - ▶ Paul lists items he would like Timothy to bring.
      - ▷ Cloak: perhaps Paul's prison was not heated and he needed to keep warm. The Mamertine prison was known for its coolness, imbedded in rock.

▷ Books... parchments: there is some debate about what Paul is referring to. He may be referring to his own writing, but he probably is referring to Scripture in some way.
▶ Like Paul, we should value God's Word, having it close to us during times of trouble, and in situations of peace and safety.

D. The apostle's godly dependence (*2 Timothy 4:14-18*)
- Despite Alexander's opposition (*2 Timothy 4:14-15*)
  ▶ Alexander is not known, but appears to have caused problems for Paul and his ministry. Alexander the Coppersmith was a constant problem who often was in Paul's prayers.
  ▶ Jesus warned that we can expect opposition when we follow Him (*John 15:18-21*).
  ▶ Alexander will be punished by God. There is comfort in knowing God will deal with those who oppose the ministry.
  ▶ Timothy is to be prepared, because Alexander (or even his followers) might disrupt the ministry in Ephesus. When Diana and other false gods/goddesses were addressed by Paul to the early believers here in Ephesus, they cast away their false idols and this Coppersmith was hurting in his pocketbook.
- Despite desertion by friends (*2 Timothy 4:16*)
  ▶ Many had abandoned Paul, not wanting to be with him when he needed their support.
  ▶ Paul forgives them, just as Jesus had forgiven others (*Luke 23:34*).
- Delighting in the Lord (*2 Timothy 4:17-18*)
  ▶ The Lord provides His servants with strength (*Luke 22:32, Hebrews 7:25*).
  ▶ This strength was so that the Gospel could go out for others to hear
  ▶ Paul was delivered from execution. The "lion" here refers to being executed by the Romans. Paul was allowed to live, and he uses this as a chance to spread the Gospel.
  ▶ Paul remains confident in God's eternal deliverance.

E. The apostle's salutation and benediction (*2 Timothy 4:19-22*)
- He sends greetings to some special brethren (*2 Timothy 4:19*)
  ▶ Priscilla and Aquila: the dynamic couple whom Paul had met on his second missionary journey (*Acts 18:1-3*).
  ▶ Onesiphorus: was one of the members of Timothy's church (*2 Timothy 1:16-18; 1 Timothy 1:3*)
- He updates Timothy on some friends (*2 Timothy 4:20*)
  ▶ Erastus: was apparently a mutual friend that remained in the church in Corinth.
  ▶ Trophimus: this man was a member of Timothy's church (*Acts 21:29*) and had traveled with Paul (*Acts 20:4*).
- He urges Timothy to see him before the winter season (*2 Timothy 4:21*)
  ▶ Paul was hoping to see Timothy again before winter came.
  ▶ This may be because winter would make it more difficult to travel, or it may have been that Paul was uncertain if he would live long enough to see Timothy.
- He sends greetings to Timothy from some special brethren (*2 Timothy 4:21*)

NOTES

NOTES

- ▶ Paul lists greetings from fellow Christians. We do not know anything about them apart from their mention here.
- ▶ For Paul, the distance that separated them did not matter. All Christians are part of a larger family, and therefore should see themselves as part of God's Church no matter where they are in the world.
- He requests the Lord's blessing on Timothy (*2 Timothy 4:22*)
    - ▶ Paul concludes his letter by asking for grace.
    - ▶ In Greek, the word "you" is plural.
        - ▷ This means that Paul is speaking to the whole church.
        - ▷ Letters such as these would often be read to the entire church.[37]

Questions

Who will you stay in contact with when this training is finished? If there are also church planters in your village or area can you fellowship together?

Take time to connect with other church planters that are working near you. Set out a plan to meet together for fellowship, accountability, and growth together in Christ! Make a note of your plans below:

THE TIMOTHY INITIATIVE

Section 3: Titus

NOTES

Chapter Fifteen
Book Outlines and Titus 1

Book Overview:

Chapter 1
The character of God's leaders ....Integrity

Chapter 2
Responsibilities in the body ....Relationships

Chapter 3
Godly living ....Character

General Outline of Titus

Theme: Sound doctrine leads to good works.

1. The responsibilities of elders in the church (*Chapter 1*)

    A. The purpose of Paul's apostleship (*Titus 1:1-4*)

    B. The command to organize and appoint (*Titus 1:5*)

    C. The moral and personal qualifications of elders (*Titus 1:6-8*)

    D. The doctrinal qualifications of elders (*Titus 1:9-16*)

2. The responsibilities of believers to each other (*Chapter 2*)

    A. Responsibilities of the old (*Titus 2:1-5*)

    B. Responsibilities of the young (*Titus 2:6*)

    C. Responsibilities of Titus for his own life (*Titus 2:7-8*)

    D. Responsibilities of Christian servants (*Titus 2:9-10*)

    E. Responsibilities concerning the grace of God (*Titus 2:11-15*)

3. The responsibilities of believers to the world (*Chapter 3*)

    A. Responsibilities to government (*Titus 3:1*)

    B. Responsibilities to all men (*Titus 3:2-8*)

C. Responsibilities toward heretics and those who create arguments (*Titus 3:9-11*)

D. Paul's personal concerns (*Titus 3:12-15*)

Specific Outline of Titus

1. The responsibilities of elders in the church (*Chapter 1*)

    A. The purpose of Paul's apostleship (*Titus 1:1-4*)
       - Paul's purpose (*Titus 1:1-3*)
         - ▶ To build faith and godliness among believers
         - ▶ To fulfill God's promise of eternal life
       - Paul's son in the faith (*Titus 1:4*)

    B. The command to organize and appoint (*Titus 1:5*)
       - Organize the churches
       - Appoint qualified elders

    C. The moral and personal qualifications of elders (*Titus 1:6-8*)
       - Household relationships (*Titus 1:6*)
         - ▶ Husband of one wife
         - ▶ The father of believing and behaving children
       - Personal character (*Titus 1:7*)
         - ▶ Above reproach
         - ▶ Not self-willed
         - ▶ Not quick-tempered
         - ▶ Not addicted to wine
         - ▶ Not too tough
         - ▶ Not fond of immoral gain
       - Christian virtues (*Titus 1:8*)
         - ▶ Hospitable
         - ▶ Lover of good
         - ▶ Sensible
         - ▶ Just
         - ▶ Devout
         - ▶ Self-controlled

    D. The doctrinal and pastoral qualifications of elders (*Titus 1:9-16*)
       - Faithful to the Word (*Titus 1:9*)
       - An exhorter of sound doctrine (*Titus 1:9*)
       - Able to refute errors and critics (*Titus 1:9*)
       - Able to teach and correct the deceived (*Titus 1:9*)
         - ▶ Reprove severely for the sake of sound faith
         - ▶ Teach clear discernment between the true and false
           - ▷ Pure doctrine produces pure living
           - ▷ A polluted mind and conscience is a sign of being defiled
         - ▶ Unbelieving lives reveal defiled hearts

NOTES

2. The responsibilities of believers to each other (*Chapter 2*)

    A. Responsibilities of the old (*Titus 2:1-3*)
- The older men (*Titus 2:1-2*)
  - Temperate, dignified and sensible
  - Sound in faith, love and perseverance
- The older women (*Titus 2:3*)
  - Reverent in their behavior
  - Not gossipers
  - Not enslaved to much wine
  - Teachers of young women

    B. Responsibilities of the young (*Titus 2:4-6*)
- The younger women (*Titus 2:4-5*)
  - To be loving wives and mothers
  - To be sensible and pure
  - To be industrious homemakers and kind
  - To be subject to their husbands for the sake of the Gospel
- The younger men (*Titus 2:6*)
  - To be sensible
  - To follow the example of Titus

    C. Responsibilities of Titus for his own life (*Titus 2:7-8*)
- Be an example of good works (*Titus 2:7*)
- Be pure in doctrine
- Be dignified
- Be beyond reproach through sound speech (*Titus 2:8*)

    D. Responsibilities of Christian servants (*Titus 2:9-10*)
- To serve their masters well (*Titus 2:9*)
- To adorn the Gospel by simple fidelity in life (*Titus 2:10*)

    E. Responsibilities concerning the grace of God (*Titus 2:11-15*)
- The grace of God brought salvation (*Titus 2:11*)
- The grace of God brought instruction for life (*Titus 2:12*)
  - With relation to ourselves
  - With relation to others
  - With relation to God
- The grace of God brought more hope of future blessing (*Titus 2:13*)
  - We are to look for His return
  - Blessing and hope lie in His second coming
- The grace was manifested to change and purify lives (*Titus 2:14*)
  - To redeem from iniquity
  - To purify the individual life
  - To produce good works
- The grace of God is the basis of one's whole ministry (*Titus 2:15*)
  - Ministry demands speaking, exhorting and reproving with all authority
  - Do not let anyone disregard you

3. The responsibilities of believers to the world (*Chapter 3*)

    A. The responsibilities to government (*Titus 3:1*)
        - Be subject to civil authorities
        - Beware of rebellious attitudes not consistent with God's grace

    B. The responsibilities to all men (*Titus 3:2-8*)
        - Do not malign anyone (*Titus 3:2*)
        - Be considerate of all men (*Titus 3:2*)
        - Be mindful of your own past life of sin (*Titus 3:3*)
        - Be mindful of God's mercy on our behalf (*Titus 3:4-7*)
            ▶ The love and grace of God appeared in Christ
            ▶ The Holy Spirit brought regeneration and renewal
            ▶ The Holy Spirit brought cleansing
            ▶ Through Jesus we have justification
            ▶ We have been made heirs in accordance with eternal life
        - Constantly emphasize the relationship between good doctrine and good works (*Titus 3:8*)
    ▶ Believers must pursue good works
    ▶ Good works are profitable for mankind

    C. Responsibilities toward heretics and those who start arguments (*Titus 3:9-11*)
        - Avoid arguments over unimportant legal points (*Titus 3:9*)
        - Avoid the contentious who refuse Biblical admonitions (*Titus 3:10-11*)
            ▶ Do not prolong a relationship with men who argue and deny your words
            ▶ Recognize non-response of the Gospel as a sign of sinfulness

    D. Paul's personal concerns (*Titus 3:12-15*)
        - His personal requests
            ▶ Titus would meet Paul at Nicopolis for the sake of being together during winter
            ▶ Titus would aid Zenas and Apollos
            ▶ Titus would continue to emphasize the need for good works to meet the pressing needs
        - His greetings and benediction

Chapter Overview:

Titus was another of God's servants who served on the island of Crete. He was also faced with the task of organizing God's church. This letter is intended to provide him with clear instruction on how to do this well.

Titus, like Timothy, must find godly leaders for the church. This first chapter describes the characteristics of those God wants as leaders in His church.

The first chapter also describes the character of other men who are not interested in God's Truth but only in themselves. Titus is to take care not to follow the example of these men, nor allow their teachings to affect the people in his congregation.

Commentary:

A. The purpose of Paul's apostleship (*Titus 1:1-4*)
   - Paul's purpose (*Titus 1:1-3*)
     ▶ To build faith and godliness among believers (*Titus 1:1*)
       ▷ Paul identifies himself as God's servant
       ▷ Paul exists to promote faith and godliness.
         ◆ Good works are the theme of the book.
         ◆ God's chosen people are to be marked by a godly lifestyle.
     ▶ To fulfill God's promise of eternal life (*Titus 1:2-3*)
       ▷ The hope is in Jesus Christ and eternal life
       ▷ God is faithful in His promises.
       ▷ God promised eternal life "long ago." Salvation has always been God's plan.
       ▷ Paul was given the task of sharing the Gospel following his conversion in *Acts 9*.
   - Paul's son in the faith (*Titus 1:4*)
     ▶ Titus, like Timothy, is referred to by Paul as a "son in [the] faith." This was a loving term meant to encourage Titus.
     ▶ Paul opens with his usual greeting, asking for blessing and health.

B. The command to organize and appoint (*Titus 1:5*)
   - Organize the churches (*Titus 1:5*)
     ▶ Paul had left Titus in charge of the church in Crete.
     ▶ Titus is meant to "set in order" what Paul had left behind.
       ▷ The word "lacking" means that the church was not yet complete.
       ▷ This meant that Titus was in charge of helping to organize the church.
   - Appoint qualified elders (*Titus 1:5*)
     ▶ Part of this task was to appoint men who could serve as elders.
       ▷ The words "elder" and "bishop" usually mean the same thing. Paul uses both words to describe this position.
       ▷ Some say that "elder" refers to the position itself, while "bishop" refers to those who actively serve in the ministry (*Acts 20:17*). But Paul does not seem to see any difference.[38] Bishop describes how the elder can lead here, as an overseer.
     ▶ The verses that follow describe what kinds of men Titus is to look for.

C. The moral and personal qualifications of elders (*Titus 1:6-8*)
   - Household relationships (*Titus 1:6*)
     ▶ Husband of one wife (*Titus 1:6*)
       ▷ Many of the characteristics on this list are identical to those listed in Paul's letters to Timothy.
       ▷ As before, one of the first qualifications Paul lists is sexual purity. This means not looking for sexual satisfaction outside of marriage.
       ▷ *Proverbs 5:15* tells us to drink water from your own cistern, and running water from your own well.
         ◆ This means finding satisfaction in your wife.
         ◆ A godly leader does not look for pleasure outside of his wife.

- ▶ The father of believing and behaving children (*Titus 1:6*)
  - ▷ Likewise, the elder's children are expected to be well-behaved.
  - ▷ The elder's children are also expected to be believers.
  - ▷ This means that the elder's household is run in a way that the elder serves as a moral and spiritual example for his family.
- Personal character (*Titus 1:7*)
  - ▶ Blameless: this is a general term meaning that the elder is a man of good moral character. Many of the other words on this list are contained in this general term.
  - ▶ Not self-willed: this means the elder is willing to obey God and serve others rather than himself.
  - ▶ Not quick-tempered: elders will face difficulty. He therefore must not be given to anger.
  - ▶ Not addicted to wine: elders must avoid overindulgence in wine and alcohol.
  - ▶ Not violent: the elder must not be a person who gets into fights or hits others.
  - ▶ Not greedy for money: the elder must place value in God rather than material possessions.
- Christian virtues (*Titus 1:8*)
  - ▶ Hospitable: the elder must be friendly and on good terms with the people he's leading.
  - ▶ Lover of good: he must love the things that God loves, and his character must mirror the things that He loves.
  - ▶ Sober-minded: this means he is "sensible," and does not become overly emotional, which can lead to poor decisions.
  - ▶ Just: the elder is fair in his dealings. He does not show favorites to those in the congregation.
  - ▶ Holy: the elder is a man of God, who daily reads the Scriptures and spends time in prayer.
  - ▶ Self-controlled: the elder is not the type of man who gives into sin easily. His lifestyle reveals his devotion to God.

D. The doctrinal and pastoral qualifications of elders (*Titus 1:9-16*)
  - Faithful to the Word (*Titus 1:9*)
    - ▶ The elder must be committed to the Gospel of Jesus Christ.
    - ▶ This means that he does not turn aside to pursue false doctrines or teachings.
  - An exhorter of sound doctrine (*Titus 1:9*)
    - ▶ The elder must also be one who promotes this good doctrine.
    - ▶ This means that the elder must have the ability to teach (*1 Timothy 3:2*).
  - Able to refute errors and critics (*Titus 1:9-12*)
    - ▶ The elder must be able to answer critics and false teachers.

NOTES

NOTES

Questions

Are you able to confront those who say the gospel is not the truth? What is one error you have had to confront in your ministry so far? How did you handle it?

- ▶ Peter tells his readers to *"always be ready to give a defense to everyone who asks you a reason for the hope that is in you."* (*1 Peter 3:15*)
- ▶ There are false teachers who are deceiving the congregation.
  - ▷ Titus needs to be mindful of those who are of the circumcision. These are the Jews who lived on Crete.
  - ▷ These Jews insisted that Gentiles had to follow Jewish tradition. But this was not the Gospel, which teaches that Jews and Gentiles can be saved through Christ alone, not from the law (*Romans 3:28*).
- ▶ These men are greedy and teaching these things in order to make money.
- ▶ The things they say are untrue, and unkind. Their teaching is insulting to the people of Crete. The Gospel is told through love and kindness, never through insulting words.
- Able to teach and correct the deceived (*Titus 1:13-16*)
  - ▶ Reprove severely for the sake of sound faith (*Titus 1:13*)
    - ▷ The false teaching is a serious problem because it is leading people away from the Truth of the Gospel.
    - ▷ Therefore it must be confronted. It is not about punishing the false teachers; it is about protecting the people that are hurt from these false teachings.
  - ▶ Teach clear discernment between the true and false doctrines (*Titus 1:14-16*)
    - ▷ A polluted mind and conscience is a sign of being defiled (*Titus 1:15*)
      - ◆ Pure doctrine produces pure character.
      - ◆ Immoral behavior is a sign of bad doctrine.
    - ▷ Unbelieving lives reveal defiled hearts (*Titus 1:16*)
      - ◆ Those who claim to know sGod may still show immoral behavior.
        - → This behavior is worthless to God.
        - → Those who practice good works in the Holy Spirit are useful for God's kingdom.
        - → This immoral behavior shows that they are not truly devoted to God's Gospel.[39]

Chapter Sixteen
The Responsibility of Believers to Each Other (Titus 2)

Chapter Overview:

God's church is meant to be a family. Older generations are to be looked at with the same respect that one gives to his/her parents. This means that your behavior matches your beliefs. This chapter describes the proper conduct of these older generations, who can be a blessing to the rest of the church.

Likewise, younger people are also to serve as leaders and examples in the church. Women have a special duty to the home and to other young women.

Slaves are to be obedient to their masters. Paul is not approving of Roman slavery, but he is saying that slaves can show their good works to slave owners so that they might see the power of the Gospel to change lives and hearts.

Finally, these things are based on the grace of God. God has been so gracious with us, we must respond in loving obedience.

Commentary:

- A. Responsibilities of the old (*Titus 2:1-3*)
  - The older men (*Titus 2:1-2*)
    - ▶ Temperate, dignified and sensible (*Titus 2:2*)
      - ▷ Actions reveal the commitment to sound doctrine (*Psalm 119:11, Proverbs 23:7, Romans 12:2, James 1:13-15*). Paul explains to Titus what good works to look for.
      - ▷ Older men are to be defined by their maturity, and not engage in reckless behavior.
    - ▶ Sound in faith, love and perseverance (*Titus 2:2*)
      - ▷ Likewise, they are to have a life that is consistent. They are to show a long-term commitment to the Gospel and to God's Word.
      - ▷ These things show the maturity of the older men. Therefore, these men serve as examples for the younger men of the church to follow.
  - The older women (*Titus 2:3*)
    - ▶ Reverent in their behavior: older women show maturity through their actions. This is probably a summary of the other qualities that follow.
    - ▶ Not gossipers: women show maturity by not spreading rumors about other people or speaking poorly of them.
    - ▶ Not given to much wine: women, like men, are not to overindulge in wine and alcohol.
    - ▶ Teachers of young women: older women are to become the examples for younger women to follow, and they teach the younger women about matters of doctrine and moral conduct.

B. Responsibilities of the young (*Titus 2:4-6*)
- The younger women (*Titus 2:4-5*)
  - ▶ To be loving wives and mothers (*Titus 2:4*)
    - ▷ The word "admonish" means to give advice.
    - ▷ Young women are to find a role in the home. This doesn't mean this is the only place for a woman, but that Paul places high value on the home life.
    - ▷ The love of a woman for her husband means that she shows a deep commitment to him. Men in the church need the support of strong families.
  - ▶ To be sensible and pure (*Titus 2:5*)
    - ▷ "Discreet" means that she is sensible, meaning she makes good, wise decisions.
    - ▷ "Chaste" means that she is pure. She does not engage in immoral behavior, but shows her faith through her good works.
  - ▶ To be industrious homemakers and kind (*Titus 2:5*)
    - ▷ The woman finds a place to serve in the home.
    - ▷ The purpose of this is so that the Word of God is not dishonored.
      - ◆ When the older women teach the younger to follow their example, it means that younger generations will lead lives of integrity and good works.
      - ◆ Since women are mothers, they have the role of raising future generations of both men and women.
  - ▶ To be subject to their husbands for the sake of the Gospel (*Titus 2:5*)
    - ▷ Taking care of the home is a means of supporting her husband.
    - ▷ A woman's actions and character reveal her moral character and also the Gospel she believes.
- The younger men (*Titus 2:6*)
  - ▶ To be sensible (*Titus 2:6*)
    - ▷ "Likewise:" just as the women were held to certain standards, so the young men were expected to display godly character.
    - ▷ "Sober-minded" means to be sensible. Young men must make wise decisions.
  - ▶ To follow the example of Titus (*Titus 2:6*)
    - ▷ Young men must follow the leadership of older men in the church.
    - ▷ Therefore Titus must show good character so that the young men will follow his example.

C. Responsibilities of Titus for his own life (*Titus 2:7-8*)
- Be an example of good works (*Titus 2:7*): Titus' life must reflect the character of the One he follows.
- Be pure in doctrine (*Titus 2:7*): Titus must remain faithful to the Gospel he preaches.
- Be dignified (*Titus 2:7*): "reverent" means to be a respectable man, who takes God and His Word seriously.
- Be beyond reproach through sound speech (*Titus 2:8*): this is a general term, meaning that others should not find anything wrong in Titus' life. He is to be a good example to the other men in the church.

NOTES

Question

What kind of example have you been to those around you? Do you focus on training up those younger than you? Discuss.

    D. Responsibilities of Christian servants (*Titus 2:9, 10*)
- To serve their masters well (*Titus 2:9*)
  - Roughly half the men in the church worked as Roman slaves.
  - Paul encourages Titus to teach these men to serve well in their jobs.
    - This is spoken of elsewhere. In *Colossians*, Paul says:
      - *Colossians 3:22-24, "Bondservants, obey in all things your masters according to the flesh, not with eyeservice, as menpleasers, but in sincerity of heart, fearing God. And whatever you do, do it heartily, as to the Lord and not to men, knowing that from the Lord you will receive the reward of the inheritance; for you serve the Lord Christ."*
    - Christians are meant to be an example to outsiders. The ultimate purpose, of course, is so that unbelievers can learn about the grace of God and come to know Christ by seeing your example.
  - Good Christian character will be an influence to those in the unbelieving world.
  - Slaves should therefore serve their masters well, without arguing, complaining or stealing from them.
- To adorn the Gospel by simple fidelity in life (*Titus 2:10*)
  - Titus must encourage his church to show faith through their works.
  - "All things" means that in every place of life, God's glory is revealed through the actions of those who claim to love Him.
  - Jesus says: "Let your light so shine before men, that they may see your good works and glorify your Father in heaven" (*Matthew 5:16*).

    E. Responsibilities concerning the grace of God (*Titus 2:11-15*)
- The grace of God brought salvation (*Titus 2:11*)
  - God's grace saved man. Not works (*Ephesians 2:8-9*).
  - God's grace "appeared:" in the person of Jesus (*John 1:17*).
- The grace of God brought instruction for life (*Titus 2:12*)
  - With relation to ourselves (*Titus 2:12*)
    - To deny ungodliness. This means to not want to pursue immoral thoughts or actions.
    - To deny worldly desires. This means to be free from the love of money or material possessions.
  - With relation to others (*Titus 2:12*)
    - Live sensibly: to make wise decisions.
    - Live righteously: to do good works.
  - With relation to God (*Titus 2:12*)
    - To live godly lives: for their character to show their relationship to God.

- ▷ The "present age" means the age we live in. For Paul it meant from the time of writing the letter to the time of Christ's return.
- The grace of God brought more hope of future blessing (*Titus 2:13*)
  - ▶ We are to look for His return (*Titus 2:13*)
    - ▷ Paul moves from the "present age" to the one to come.
    - ▷ Christians are to long for Christ's return, when all things are made new.
  - ▶ Blessing and hope are in His Second Coming (*Titus 2:13*)
    - ▷ Christ's return will restore creation (*Revelation 20-21*).
    - ▷ Christians must therefore look forward to the day of Christ's return.
- The grace was manifested to change and purify lives (*Titus 2:14*)
  - ▶ To redeem from iniquity (*Titus 2:14*)
    - ▷ Christ came to save us from sin.
    - ▷ The cross is the way Christ offers forgiveness (*John 3:16*).
    - ▷ "Every lawless deed" refers to all of man's sinful behavior.
  - ▶ To purify the individual life (*Titus 2:14*)
    - ▷ Humanity is made pure through Christ's sacrifice (*Isaiah 53:5*) when we accept Him as our Savior and God.
    - ▷ The purpose of redemption was so that Christians could become God's people.
  - ▶ To produce good works (*Titus 2:14*)
    - ▷ Salvation also produces good works (*Philippians 1:6*).
    - ▷ Good works reveal the Truth of Jesus who saved us from our sin.
- The grace of God is the basis of one's whole ministry (*Titus 2:15*)
  - ▶ Ministry demands speaking, exhorting and reproving with all authority (*Titus 2:15*)
    - ▷ Grace must be the main focus of all Christian ministry.
    - ▷ Authority is found not in man's wisdom, but through God's Spirit Who will lead us into all Truth (*John 16:13*).
  - ▶ Do not let anyone disregard you (*Titus 2:15*)
    - ▷ To "disregard" means to ignore or not respect.
    - ▷ Christians should not argue with others, but their conduct should show people that God's grace is not something that can be ignored.[40]

Chapter Seventeen
The Responsibility of Believers to the World (Titus 3)

Chapter Overview:

Godly leaders must live in submission to the government. Titus' city had a history of people refusing the authority of the Roman government. But as Christians, they had a unique responsibility to obey their leaders and serve them with humble obedience. The church was called to live differently than the city of Crete. This should lead to city change as believers are the salt of a city.

Salvation in Christ is not based on works, but only on God's grace through Jesus. There were false teachers in the church who were teaching that Christians must obey the law and be circumcised. But this was not the Gospel that Paul had taught, and salvation could never come by what you do, but only by what Christ has done.

Christians are to avoid conflict with false teachers. The Gospel will unite congregations, but arguments will only divide them. The Gospel is the most valuable thing; therefore time should not be wasted in arguing with these false teachers.

Commentary:

A. The responsibilities to government (*Titus 3:1*)
   - Be subject to civil authorities (*Titus 3:1*)
     ▶ There was a history of men in Crete resisting Roman government.
     ▶ Paul encouraged obedience to those in authority (*Romans 13:1-8*).
   - Beware of rebellious attitudes not consistent with God's grace (*Titus 3:1*)
     ▶ Some may wish to rebel against the government.
     ▶ Paul encourages them to be prepared for "every good deed." The purpose was not to try and change the government, but to show them the truth of Jesus through humble obedience and good works.

B. The responsibilities to all men (*Titus 3:2-8*)
   - Do not malign anyone (*Titus 3:2*): this means not insulting others or gossiping about others.
   - Be uncontentious (*Titus 3:2*): this means not being eager to start fights and arguments.
   - Be gentle (*Titus 3:2*): this means to be kind to others around them, displaying humility.
   - Be considerate of all men (*Titus 3:2*): this means to treat others with the same kindness shown to you by God (*Matthew 7:12*).
   - Be mindful of your own past life of sin (*Titus 3:3*)
     ▶ Foolish: sinners lack God's wisdom.
     ▶ Disobedient: sinners cannot obey God.

- ▸ Deceived: sinners are trapped into thinking their way is right (*Proverbs 16:9*).
- ▸ Enslaved to various lusts: sinners are trapped in lives of sin. They cannot on their own escape from sin.
- ▸ Spending life in malice and envy: sinners are in poor relationships with others, feeling jealous of others and hating them for their deeds.
- ▸ Ruled by hate: sinners do not have the love of God, and therefore are ruled by hatred and envy.
- Be mindful of God's mercy on our behalf (*Titus 3:4-7*)
  - ▸ The love and grace of God appeared in Christ (*Titus 3:4*)
    - ▷ Christ revealed God's kindness
    - ▷ Christ revealed God's love
  - ▸ The Holy Spirit brought rebirth and renewal (*Titus 3:5*)
    - ▷ Salvation is by grace alone, not works. It is a gift from God (*Romans 6:23*).
    - ▷ The Holy Spirit is the One Who brings new life and salvation.
  - ▸ Through Jesus we have justification (*Titus 3:6-7*)
    - ▷ The Spirit came through Jesus (*John 20:22*).
    - ▷ Justification means to be viewed as righteous before God (*Romans 5:1-9*).
  - ▸ We have been made heirs in accordance with eternal life (*Titus 3:7*).
    - ▷ Those who are justified in Christ are promised to reign with Him.
    - ▷ To be an 'heir' means to have the promise of receiving God's Kingdom.
    - ▷ Christians are promised a rich blessing in God's future Kingdom (*1 Peter 3:7*).
- Constantly emphasize the relationship between good doctrine and good works (*Titus 3:8*)
  - ▸ Believers must pursue good works (*Titus 3:8*)
    - ▷ Titus is encouraged to emphasize the need for good works.
    - ▷ Good works show the world the reality of the Gospel and its power to change lives.
  - ▸ Good works are profitable for mankind (*Titus 3:8*)
    - ▷ Good works benefit others.
      - ◆ Good works help others by serving their needs.
      - ◆ Good works help others by pointing them to the Gospel, which can save them.
    - ▷ Therefore, Christians must take care to practice good works so that others can see the power of the Gospel.

NOTES

Question

How can you teach the importance of good works and still be clear that salvation is by faith alone? Discuss.

NOTES

C. Responsibilities toward false teachers and those who start arguments (*Titus 3:9-11*)
- Avoid arguments over unimportant legal points (*Titus 3:9*)
  - False teachers often start arguments over unimportant matters.
    - "Foolish disputes, genealogies, contentions, and strivings about the law" all refer to arguments about ideas other than the Gospel.
    - False teachers were good students in the wrong things. Their learning was worthless compared to the Gospel.
  - Christians should stick to the Gospel rather than trying to win arguments.
- Avoid the contentious who refuse Biblical admonitions (*Titus 3:10-11*)
  - Do not prolong a relationship with men who argue and deny your words (*Titus 3:10*)
    - Christians must be on good terms with unbelievers (*Colossians 4:2-6*).
    - But Christians should not involve themselves with men who only want to argue.
      - Warn them.
      - Warn them again.
      - Then avoid them.
    - The purpose was not to reject others, but to make sure that Christians spend their time wisely and share the Gospel, not getting stuck in long arguments that do not serve anyone.
  - Recognize non-response of the Gospel as a sign of sinfulness (*Titus 3:11*)
    - *"For everyone practicing evil hates the light and does not come to the light, lest his deeds should be exposed."* (*John 3:20*)
    - Those who do not accept the Gospel do so because they prefer their sin to God's Truth.
    - This means that God does not reject sinners. God simply allows sinners to have their own way.

D. Paul's personal concerns (*Titus 3:12-15*)
- His personal requests (*Titus 3:12-14*)
  - Titus would meet Paul at Nicopolis for the sake of being together during winter (*Titus 3:12*)
    - Artemas: a mutual friend of Paul and Titus.
    - Tychius: one of Paul's assistants (*Acts 20:4, Ephesians 6:21, Colossians 4:7, 2 Timothy 4:12*)
    - Paul and Titus would be together at winter. Titus would leave the church in the hands of the elders.
  - Titus would aid Zenas and Apollos (*Titus 3:13*)
    - Zenas: a friend of Paul.
    - Apollos: a fellow worker of Paul (*Acts 18:24, 1 Corinthians 1:12*) and dynamic preacher of the Word of God.
  - Titus would continue to emphasize the need for good works to meet the pressing needs (*Titus 3:14*)
    - "Urgent needs" refers to the unrest within the church and the need to teach Christians to live lives according to the Gospel.
    - God's people must learn to practice good works.

- ▷ Goal was to be "fruitful."
  - ◆ This means displaying good deeds.
  - ◆ This also means to produce Christian disciples.
- His greetings and benediction (*Titus 3:15*)
  - ▶ Paul greets everyone at Titus' church. "Those who love us" refer to friends and fellow Christians in the church.
  - ▶ Paul wishes them all grace.[41]

THE TIMOTHY INITIATIVE

SECTION 4: ADDITIONAL RESOURCES

Chapter Eighteen
Suggestions for Preaching

The following section explores ways to apply principles from the Pastoral letters to your life as well as providing suggestions on how to teach these books to your new church.

1. Personal Application

A. Personal life
- Love others (*1 Timothy 1:5*)
  - ▶ The goal is not to simply know God's Truth, but to live it.
  - ▶ Love is the final goal. To whom are you showing love?
- Personal Integrity
  - ▶ Greed (*1 Timothy 3:3, 3:8, 6:9-10, Titus 1:7, 1:11*)
    - ▷ Christians must not be controlled by money.
    - ▷ God will bless His followers, but He will seldom make them rich.
    - ▷ Money can be a blessing to others by giving it away.
    - ▷ A relationship with God will show how money can be used for God's kingdom.
  - ▶ Sexual purity (*1 Timothy 3:2, Titus 1:6*)
    - ▷ Sexual satisfaction should not be found outside of marriage.
    - ▷ Avoid sexual temptation.
    - ▷ Find accountability.
      - ◆ Other Christian men struggle with this.
      - ◆ Confess sins to one another and hold one another accountable for your actions.
  - ▶ Gentle attitude (*1 Timothy 3:2-3, Titus 1:8*)
    - ▷ Godly leaders do not start arguments or fights.
    - ▷ Avoid raising your voice.
    - ▷ Do your best to be a friend to everyone.
  - ▶ Alcohol (*1 Timothy 3:3, Titus 1:7*)
    - ▷ Alcohol can control you.
    - ▷ Some may avoid being controlled by alcohol by never drinking it.
  - ▶ Forgiving (*2 Timothy 3:10*)
    - ▷ Forgive others easily. Tell them that they are forgiven.
    - ▷ Do not hold their wrongs against them. Once they are forgiven, make a plan to never speak of the issue again.
- Prayer (*1 Timothy 2:8*)
  - ▶ Pray as often as you can.
  - ▶ Set time aside each day for prayer.
  - ▶ Pray for others. You may wish to write down names and things to pray for throughout the day, so that you can later bring these items to the Lord in prayer.
- Discipline (*2 Timothy 2:1-7*)
  - ▶ Be a good student of God's Word. Study daily.
  - ▶ As with prayer, it is helpful to have a schedule of time in which to read and study the Bible.

- Be a humble servant (*1 Timothy 4:6*)
  - ▶ Serve others.
  - ▶ Look for needs in friends and family and do them without asking.
    - ▷ For example, you can clean their home for them.
    - ▷ You can agree to help with a difficult project.
    - ▷ Invite guests to your home to share a meal.
  - ▶ Expect nothing in return. Only seek to show the love of Jesus with friends and neighbors.

B. Home life
- Honor your wife (*1 Timothy 3:4*)
  - ▶ Wives have a special duty in the home. Thank her for her kindness and her service.
  - ▶ Treat your wife with respect. She is not a servant; she is your partner in ministry. Show her the same love and respect that she shows you.
  - ▶ Tell her you love her. Wives will enjoy their husbands showing this type of love.
- Teach your children well (*Titus 1:6*)
  - ▶ Good character.
    - ▷ Be sure your life reflects godly character. Children will model the behavior shown by their parents.
    - ▷ Teach children right from wrong, based on the Gospel and the whole counsel of God.
    - ▷ Children will grow to become godly men and women
  - ▶ Love the Gospel (*2 Timothy 4:2*)
    - ▷ Teach your children the Gospel.
    - ▷ Help them grow in maturity by teaching from the Scriptures.
      - ◆ This means developing discipline in them just as you have yourself.
      - ◆ Some families have daily times when they meet together to read Scripture. Perhaps before each dinner, the family can sit to read together and pray.
- Show respect to older family (*Titus 2:1-10, 1 Timothy 5:1-16*)
  - ▶ Some homes will contain older family members.
  - ▶ Respect older family members as members of the family.
  - ▶ Listen to their advice and respect their wisdom.

C. Work life
- Work hard as for God (*Titus 2:9*)
  - ▶ Realize your job isn't about the money.
  - ▶ Work at your job as if you were working for God.
- Serve well (*Titus 2:9*)
  - ▶ Serve others well in your job.
  - ▶ Be cheerful. Do every task without complaining.
  - ▶ Serving with excellence and a good attitude displays the power of the Gospel in our lives and draws others to faith in Christ.
- Look for opportunities to share your faith with others.

D. Church life
- Be a leader (*1 Timothy 3:1*)
  - Churches need men to take leadership within the church.
  - Leadership must be something that you desire.
- Avoid fights and arguments (*Titus 3:9*)
  - The church cannot be divided by arguments and issues that take the focus off of the Gospel.
  - Do not be distracted by arguments or foolish words.
- Be gentle (*1 Timothy 3:2-3, Titus 1:8*)
  - God's people must be kind and forgiving to one another.
  - This gentleness can often be more powerful than any argument.
- Be devoted to the Bible (*2 Timothy 2:15, 4:2*)
  - Avoid the kinds of false teachings in the church by focusing the ministry on the Gospel contained in Scripture.
  - Be sure to understand the Bible so it can be taught correctly to the congregation.
- Teach others (*2 Timothy 2:24*)
  - Churches must be places where Christians can come and learn about God.
  - Church leaders must therefore be those who teach God's Truth to others.
- Gently correct false doctrine (*1 Timothy 6:1-10, 2 Timothy 4:5*)
  - Do not tolerate false teachers, but be patient as well.
  - The purpose of correcting them is not to be proven right, but so that the false teachers can be restored to fellowship in the eyes of God and in the local church.
- Persevere (*2 Timothy 4:5*)
  - Ministry is difficult. It will be tempting to give up.
  - We are called to remain faithful despite times of trouble and persecution.

2. How to Preach to the Church

A. Preach the Gospel (*2 Timothy 4:2*)
- Teach the Gospel clearly in the church.
  - Find every opportunity to teach the Gospel.
  - Communion is a convenient time to share the Gospel.
- Teach the church that God's people are devoted to His Gospel.
- Teach grace, not works.
  - It is tempting to try and earn salvation based on works.
  - Teach congregations that salvation is based on the cross, not works of the law.

B. Teach good character (*1 Timothy 2:9-15, 2 Timothy 2:1-10, Titus 2:1-15*)
- Show no tolerance for sin.
- Promote good Christian character.
  - Identify places within the church where the standards of elders are not met.
    - Teach on what Jesus' attitude and personal life was like while He was on earth.

- Teach connection between good doctrine and good works. (*Titus 3:5*)
  ▶ Good belief leads to good actions.
  ▶ God expects good works.
  ▶ Good works are a form of evangelism or pre-evangelism.

C. Identify false teaching (*1 Timothy 1:8-11, 4:1-5, 2 Timothy 3:1-9, Titus 1:10-16, 3:8*)
  - Determine what false teachings are affecting the congregation.
    ▶ For example, are there those who teach that God will only help them get rich?
    ▶ Are people turning aside from good teaching for other teachings?
  - Warn them about these teachings.
    ▶ Describe the content of these teachings.
    ▶ Describe how the Gospel is different.
    ▶ Describe the character of these false teachers.
  - Make clear that what is popular or pleasing is not always true.
    ▶ Some false teachings may be attractive.
    ▶ Truth is determined by God, not what is pleasing to men.

D. Encourage leadership (*1 Timothy 3:1*)
  - Encourage men in the congregation to pursue positions of leadership within the church.
  - Publicly recognize leaders and servants in the church.
    ▶ Ask leaders to appear before the congregation.
    ▶ Specifically name the contributions of these servants and leaders, so that others may appreciate their example of love and service.
  - Speak of the eternal rewards of service to God.
  - Do not ignore the difficulties leaders will face.
    ▶ Encourage leaders to be faithful during these times.
    ▶ Emphasize God's power in equipping God's people for every good work.
  - Teach humble service
    ▶ Teach on the servanthood of Jesus.
    ▶ Encourage the church to follow this example

E. Teach against greed (*1 Timothy 3:3, 8; 6:9-10, Titus 1:7, 1:11*)
  - The love of money is destructive
    ▶ It is based on selfish motives.
    ▶ Greed leads to other sins in an effort to obtain more.
  - Teach that God provides for the material needs of those faithful to Him.
  - Encourage giving.
    ▶ Money can be used to bless others.
    ▶ Giving money away prevents us from being enslaved to it.

F. Teach gratitude (*1 Timothy 3:3, 8; 6:9-10, Titus 1:7, 1:11*)
  - Greed always wants more. Gratitude means being content with what God has already given.
  - Encourage the church to find things that God has blessed them with.
  - Teach thankfulness as part of our prayer life.

NOTES

G. Teach them to honor family (*1 Timothy 2:9-15, Titus 2:1-8*)
- Stress the value of wives to the life of the home.
- Encourage families to teach God's Word to their children.
- Teach husbands and wives to model moral character to their children.
- Teach sexual purity.
    ▶ Married men should not find satisfaction in women other than their wives.
    ▶ Single men should not find satisfaction outside of marriage.

H. Teach perseverance (*2 Timothy 3:10-14*)
- Teach the church that hard times cannot be avoided.
- Show them the examples of Paul and Jesus being persecuted.
- Teach that the sufferings are only temporary, but that we can find hope in the return of Christ.

I. Submission to authority (*Titus 3:1-4*)
- Our rulers are appointed by God.
- Our response to the government should be submission and obedience.
    ▶ Submission to authorities is a form of Christian service.
    ▶ Submission to authorities is an example of faith for outsiders to see the life-changing power of the Gospel.

J. Teach the Bible (*2 Timothy 2:15, 3:16, 4:2*)
- Some teachers rely on clever stories or ideas to try and appeal to the people they teach.
- Godly leaders teach their church to love God's Word
    ▶ Teach the value of discipline and study.
        ▷ Teach the church how to study the Bible.
        ▷ Encourage the church to engage in regular Bible study and personal devotion.
    ▶ Teach on the life-changing nature of God's Word.
    ▶ Encourage families to value the Word together.

K. Encourage togetherness (*2 Timothy 4:19-22*)
- Teach on the value of godly relationships.
    ▶ These relationships are valuable during times of difficulty and persecution.
    ▶ These relationships can improve the quality of our service and Christian ministry.
- Encourage the people in your local church to spend time together.

L. Enjoy God-focused worship (*1 Timothy 2:8*)
- Pray together as a church
    ▶ Take time to thank God for the gifts He has generously given to His people.
    ▶ Encourage the church to be in prayer for themselves.
- Worship God joyfully.[42]

Chapter Nineteen
Godly Leaders

Church leaders (elders and deacons) are called to be of righteous character.

The culture that surrounds the church might be the complete opposite of righteousness! This may include gambling, alcohol and women.

This means that church leaders must be the same person in and outside of the church. They must not display these godly qualities on Sunday morning or your main worship time(s) and get drunk on the other days of the week.

This means that there may be times when church leaders wisely avoid parts of town that may cause them to sin.

Commentary:

1. Godly Leaders Understand the Proper Use of Money (*Titus 1:7, 11*)

   A. The danger of greed
   - Greed
     - Greed is the desire for more.
     - Greed will lead to other, immoral actions.
     - Greed shows a lack of trust in God.

   B. Contentment
   - Contentment means being happy with what God has already provided.
   - A life of contentment will be shown through a life of thankfulness toward God.

   C. Good stewards of money
   - Using it for your basic needs.
   - Giving it away to those in need.
   - God provides the wisdom for financial stewardship.

   D. Gifts for the Pastor(s)
   - Some men may desire to offer gifts to the pastors and elders. But these men might also be doing so in order to offer bribes. The pastor takes the gift, but is then expected to do something in return. Be careful of giving people entitlement.
   - Pastors should be willing to accept gifts, but not without asking why the gift was given or who the gift is from.
   - Pastors may have to refuse gifts from people they feel may be trying to manipulate them and the church for their own political ends.

   E. Church leaders who rule well are deserving to receive money and gifts for their sacrificial service.

NOTES

- Many areas are too poor to offer money or valuable possessions to their leaders. Church leaders may be forced to do without money coming in on a regular basis.
- Poor communities may find ways to honor their leaders by sharing food or services for one another.
- Those who are wealthy may show God's love by providing for those who are less fortunate. This is in order to share the love of God and the Gospel. Many neighbors may not know Jesus. Sharing Christ's love through service can be a way to open a door for evangelism.

2. Other Religions

A. It is very likely that other religions will exist in the same area as the church.
   - Those who come to know Jesus must reject their former religions. Christians cannot serve both their former religion and the Gospel. However, new believers must work hard at maintaining relationships when possible for the sake of love and compassion.
   - Rejecting a former religion may result in persecution.

B. There may be those who wish to keep their faith in Jesus a secret to avoid persecution. This may help to protect their families from becoming targets of violence by those who oppose the Truth. While we may understand this behavior, these people are not good choices for church leadership. A church leader cannot keep his faith a secret. Using wisdom is one thing, keeping Jesus and your relationship with Him a secret is another.
   - Church leaders can work to provide greater acceptance of Christianity so that people no longer feel forced to keep their faith a secret.
   - Christians may need to open their households to those who are kicked out of their own house for becoming Christians.

3. Godly Leaders are Disciplined in Study and Prayer
(2 Timothy 2:1-6, 2:15, 3:16-17, Titus 1:9)

A. Study
   - A godly leader is committed to a lifetime of studying the Word of God.
   - Studying must be done with accuracy.
   - Bible study can provide leaders with an understanding of good and holy character.
   - Bible study improves a leader's ability to distinguish true and false doctrines and teachings.

B. Prayer
   - Prayer is a part of a leader's personal life
      ▶ Leaders pray often.
         ▷ All will benefit from setting aside regular time for prayer.
         ▷ God desires frequent prayers.
         ▷ "Mastering the art of prayer, like any other art, will take time, and the amount of time we allocate to it will be the true measure of our

conception of its importance. We always find time for that which we deem most important."[43]
- ▶ Leaders pray for specific things
  - ▷ Guidance
  - ▷ Meeting others need
  - ▷ Listening to the Holy Spirit
  - ▷ Some may benefit from writing down prayer requests throughout the day so that they may pray later for those things. Journaling is a wonderful way of praise and prayer to our Father.
- ▶ Leaders also thank God
  - ▷ Prayers of thanksgiving help to fight against the temptation of greed.
  - ▷ Prayers of thankfulness promote a lifestyle of joy and gratitude.
- Prayer is also a part of church gatherings
  - ▶ Men are to have a leadership role in public gatherings of prayer.
  - ▶ Prayer is to be a part of public worship.
  - ▶ Prayer is done in a state of purity.
    - ▷ Demands confession of sin.
    - ▷ Forgiveness of our brothers and sisters takes place.

4. Godly Leaders Promote Healthy Church Leadership (*Titus 1:5*)

- ❖ Promote a desire for leadership
  - Godly leadership must be seen as a desirable position in the church.
  - Godly leaders must have a desire to serve God and the people of His church.
  - Godly leaders promote this desire for leadership in others so that other leaders can be raised up for God's church.
  - "God's greatest gifts to Israel, better than the land itself, were men such as Moses and David and Isaiah. God's greatest gifts are always men; His greatest endowment to the church was the gift of twelve men trained for leadership."[44]
  - Godly leaders desire future reward for their service, not for reward in this life. If reward on earth comes that is fine, but that is not the focus… eternal rewards and the smile of God is our concern.
  - "True greatness, true leadership, is achieved not by reducing men to one's service but in giving oneself in selfless service to them. And that is never done without cost."[45]

5. Godly Leaders are First Servants

A. Jesus was and is a Servant

B. We follow His example
- Referring to John 7:37-39, J. Oswald Sanders writes: "Spiritual leadership can be exercised only by Spirit filled people. It is of more than passing significance the central qualification of those who are to occupy even subordinate positions of responsibility in the early church was that they be people 'full of the Holy Spirit.' They must be known primarily for their spirituality… Why is this so important? People who are sensitive to the

overriding leading of the Holy Spirit willingly submitted to His control, they are delighted to obey His prompting and leading… What is it to be filled with the Spirit? Reduced to its simplest term, to be filled with the Spirit means, through voluntary surrender and in response to the Holy Spirit taking control, the human personality is filled, mastered, by the Holy Spirit. To be filled with the Spirit, is to be controlled by the Spirit. Intellect and emotions and volition as well as physical powers all become available to Him for achieving the purposes of God. Under His control, natural gifts of leadership are sanctified and lifted to their highest power. The now ungrieved and unhindered Spirit is able to produce the fruit of the Spirit in the life of the leader, with added winsomeness and attractiveness in their service and with power in their witness to Christ. All service is but the outflow of the Holy Spirit through yielded and filled lives."[46]

6. Godly leaders endure difficulty (*2 Timothy 3:1-15, Titus 3:1-4*)

A. Types of difficulty
- False teachers will come into the church.
  - ▶ These men will start arguments with people in the church over doctrine.
  - ▶ These men will lead others astray through ideas that sound appealing but are not true.

B. Perseverance
- Godly leaders are those who endure times of great difficulty and remain faithful to the Gospel of God.
- Perseverance is based on the promises of God.
  - ▶ Suffering is only temporary.
  - ▶ God promises eternal salvation *and rewards* in His Kingdom to those who serve Him.

7. Godly Leaders Value Godly Relationships
(*2 Timothy 4:9, 4:19-22, Titus 2:1-8*)

A. Friendships (*2 Timothy 4:9, 19-22*)
- Godly leaders support one another during times of difficulty and encourage one another.
- Godly leaders seek one another out for support when they are struggling.

B. Church family (*Titus 2:1-8*)
- The church family will contain people from many different backgrounds.
- All members of the church family are worthy of honor.
- In some cases, there may be those inside the church who have hurt one another before they became Christians. These people must be willing to sit down and deal honestly with the hurt, willing to move forward in forgiveness.
- There will be those of us who hurt one another in the local church after we are believers. We are sinners who are covered by the blood of Jesus.

8. Godly Leaders Promote Healthy Homes (*Titus 2:1-8*)

A. Children are called to be well-behaved as well as to be Christians.
   - Education is important in raising children. Helping them learn can provide better opportunities as they grow, and these opportunities provide a better chance for the spread of the Gospel.
   - Some children will not believe. It is not the parents' job to force their children to become Christians. These children need prayer and love. They should not be thrown out of the household for their unwillingness to believe, but to be dealt with in patience and understanding, so that they may come to know Christ.

B. Likewise, older generations may be living under the same roof.
   - Not all older generations will be believers.
   - It is the Christian's responsibility to witness to everyone in his or her household. But this does not mean that others can be forced into becoming Christians. People of every generation need a great deal of love, patience and prayer.

C. Not everyone in the house will be a Christian. This can be a good thing, because it means that Christians have the wonderful opportunity to share Christ with their parents and children.

D. Wife
   - Godly leaders love and value their wives for their service in the home.
   - Godly leaders remain faithful to their wives.
     ▶ Not seeking sexual satisfaction with another woman.
     ▶ Single Christians remain sexually pure.
   - Does "husband of one wife" mean that you can't marry more than one woman?
     ▶ God intends marriage between one man and one woman.
     ▶ In the past, God has tolerated men having many wives. But this does not mean that it is proper.
     ▶ God also hates divorce. In many conditions, divorcing one's wife would leave her poor and vulnerable.
     ▶ The loving thing is to not divorce one's wife, and to no longer marry another woman. Take care of the one wife in your own household, but do not seek to add more.

E. Time Commitments:
   - Church leaders must also remain responsible towards their family. Responsibilities within the church will often take a lot of time.
   - This can take time away from taking care of family and the home. Family members often have to do more work because the elder is not able to help in the home. This is not fair to one's family. It is difficult and must be balanced.
   - Church leaders must learn to balance their time between their church and family. All of us can grow in understanding margin and boundaries in our lives.

9. Godly Leaders Respond to False Teachings
(*2 Timothy 4:3-5, Titus 3:9-11*)

A. False teachers will sometimes be hard to identify. Their teaching may sound very good, and may even attract large crowds.

B. Teaching that may temporarily sound good will often make promise of wealth and happiness. This weak thinking states that followers will become rich; they will gain a lot of possessions or have good crops and a large family.

C. God will bless those who follow Him, but these things are not to be expected or demanded of God.

D. Followers of Christ must avoid these teachers and teach their churches to do the same.

E. False teachers may be identified by their inability to match their teachings with those found in Scripture.
   - False teachers often use the Bible to try and prove their teachings are correct. But even Satan misquoted Scripture. This inability to use good hermeneutics is why we start our training with TTI in *Book 1: Biblical Hermeneutics*.
   - Christians must therefore measure false teachers by their focus on the Gospel. Good teachers teach salvation by faith alone in Jesus and His cross. Disciples take up this cross and pursue Christ's righteousness.
   - False teachers teach works — That blessings may come by doing good works. Good works are important, but only in order to spread the Gospel and bring glory to the Father.

F. False teachers must be confronted.
   - Those false teachers who do not repent are to be warned twice, then ignored and avoided.
   - Do not waste time trying to correct false teachers, but focus instead on sharing the Gospel and teaching God's Word.

10. Politics and Government

A. Obeying the Government
   - Christians must obey the government, as they are God's appointed leaders.
   - There have been times and places where the government places limits on Christian freedoms. They might forbid evangelism or preaching the Bible.
     ▶ Christians must not allow their fear of the government to prevent them from serving Jesus Christ.
     ▶ Christians must put Jesus and the Gospel first.
     ▶ In these — and only these — times, the government may be disobeyed so that the Gospel may be preached. Even here, please use discretion

and discernment, there may be another way to present the Truth in an accurate yet wiser way.

B. Political Involvement
- When able, Christians should have a voice in politics and may express their opinions on the world of politics.
- The Christian duty is to obey the government (*Romans 13*).
- But Christians are called to serve God and His Kingdom before human government.
- In some places, political protests become violent. Christians must never be associated with these types of protests and demonstrations.

11. Persecution

A. The church will be persecuted. Jesus promised that the world would hate Christians.

B. Christians must not resist persecution through violence. This may mean that Christians are forced to witness violence against their church and their family.
- Those who are persecuted must be prayed for.
- Those who are persecuted must be cared for. When able, Christians can take them food and water and pray with them.

C. Christians may remember that Christ was persecuted for us. We find hope and joy in the fact that He is coming again.[47]

APPENDIX
MARRIAGE AND FAMILY

(Written by Ken & Jackie Kendall)

C.S. Lewis once said "Love, as distinct from being in love is not merely a feeling. It is a deep unity, maintained by the will and deliberately strengthened by habit; reinforced by (in Christian marriages), the grace which both partners ask, and receive, from God."

1. Your First Congregation

A. As a married man and possibly also a father, you as a church planter have your first congregation. Your wife and family are your first church. Your family will follow you as you follow Jesus (*1 Cor. 11:1*). Whatever you want to teach your church, the demonstration begins with your family.

B. You will teach men in your church how to love their wives, as you demonstrate how God wants you to love and honor your own wife. What does the Bible say about the way a man is to love his wife? Consider the following passage of Scripture:
- *"Husbands, love your wives, just as Christ also loved the church and gave Himself for her, that He might sanctify and cleanse her with the washing of water by the word. So husbands ought to love their own wives as their own bodies; he who loves his wife loves himself. For no one ever hated his own flesh, but nourishes and cherishes it, just as the Lord does the church."* (Eph. 5:25,26,28,29)
- God is asking all men (not just the pastor but all men in your church), to love his wife; as Christ loved the church. Your wife is God's masterpiece and you are to love her and let God finish the work He has begun in her.
- As C.S. Lewis once said: "We are… a Divine work of art, something that God is making, and therefore something with which He will not be satisfied until it has a certain character."

C. Christ died for the church, in what ways can you as a man lay your life down for your wife?
- When a man is harming his wife, he is harming not only himself but also the Lord whom he loves. Have you considered that how you treat your wife is how your treat the Lord? Who is her Savior and heavenly Father as well as yours?
- *"Husbands likewise, dwell with them with understanding, giving honor to the wife, as to the weaker vessel, and as being heirs together of the grace of life, that your prayers may not be hindered."* (1 Peter 3:7, 8)
- Do you realize that your wife is a co-heir with you of the grace of life and that your mistreatment of her will hinder your prayers? As a Pastor/church planter, how you shepherd your wife will be the most powerful demonstration of God's love and power through you.
- *"The elders who are among you I exhort, I who am a fellow elder and a witness of the sufferings of Christ, and also a partaker of the glory that will be revealed: Shepherd the flock of God which is among you, serving*

as overseers, not by compulsion but willingly, nor for dishonest gain but eagerly; nor as being lords over those entrusted to you, but being examples to the flock; and when the Chief Shepherd appears, you will receive the crown of glory that does not fade away." (1 Peter 5:1-4)

Question

Read Psalm 23 and compare how you are to shepherd your wife and children and ultimately the church.

2. **Inspiring Women of the Bible**

   A. As a shepherd you can encourage not only your wife and daughters but also all the other women in your church to strive to be like many of the wonderful women in the Bible (*1 Pet. 5:1-4; John 10*).

   B. There are many women of the Bible that can inspire not only your wife and daughters but also men. The harvest is plentiful but the laborers are few (*Mat. 9:37, 38*).

   C. Have you considered the inspiration a woman can be to her husband and family?
      - **Abigail**: Wise and generous (*1 Sam. 25*)
         ▶ In *1 Sam. 25*, there is a story about a beautiful woman who was married to a very mean man. Although her husband was not a nice man, Abigails' patient kindness saved the lives of all the men who worked on her husband's land. Patient kindness can protect not only you but those around you as well. The name Abigail means, "A Father's Joy." When a woman behaves wisely and patiently, she will not only bring her heavenly Father joy but she could save lives around her. The Holy Spirit gives us the power to act wisely. Remember one of the fruits of the spirit is joy.
      - **Deborah**: Bold and courageous (*Jud. 4-5*)
         ▶ Deborah was a leader in Ephraim. Everyday she would sit under a palm tree and the people would come to her for advice. At that time the people of Israel were at war and even though they had God on their side, the people were afraid. Deborah led the army in battle, and God gave them the victory. Deborah is proof that we can conquer our fears and face difficult situations with confidence because God can help us do mighty things.
      - **Esther**: Courageous queen (*Esther*)
         ▶ As a young girl Esther won a beauty contest and her inner beauty allowed her to be chosen by the King of Persia. As the winner she was chosen as the next queen of the nation. She found favor and kindness

NOTES

with the King and was loved more than all of the other women (*Est. 2:17*).

- **Miriam**: Courageous older sister (*Num. 12*)
  ▶ When Moses was a baby, Pharaoh had sent out a decree for the killing of any Hebrew boys that were born. Moses' mother hid him for as long as she could then she had to put him in a little basket and send him down the Nile River in hopes that someone would save him. Moses' brave sister, Miriam, watched him as he floated down the Nile River. She watched the basket float right up to the palace.
  ▶ Young Miriam bravely approached the princess and offered to help with the baby who had been discovered in the basket. Miriam helped save Moses, who later led millions across the Red Sea. Miriam led the women in dancing and singing as a celebration to God after crossing the Red Sea (*Exo. 15:20, 21*).
- **Jochebed**: Mother of Moses (*Heb. 11:23*).
  ▶ Moses mother Jochebed was a woman of faith that was proven in her courage to protect her son against the King's edit to destroy all the male Hebrew children. Jochebbed's faith was considered so important that she ended up being mentioned in the famous hall of faith (*Heb. 11:23*).
- **Phoebe**: Brave Carrier of God's Word (*Rom. 16:1, 2*).
  ▶ Paul gave praise to a woman named Phoebe. Paul called Phoebe a sister, servant, saint and helper. How did Phoebe help this great apostle? She had the great responsibility of delivering a letter to the Roman church. Phoebe, a woman in the first century was a courier for a letter from Paul to the church in Rome. Phoebe carried a letter that would someday be a major letter in the New Testament. In this day, women were just not given such an honor. Phoebe was a standout disciple.

Question

Discuss men and women being trained to carry the Word of God to those in their community and their country (*Act. 1:8; Mat. 28:18, 19*).

D. Inspiring women all can follow.
- Abigail: Wise and generous (*1Sam. 25*)
- Anna: Waited on the Lord (*Luk. 2*)
- Deborah: Bold and courageous (*Jud. 4-5*)
- Mary: Said, "Whatever Lord" (*Mat. 1-2*)
- Hagar: Trusted God would take care of her (*Gen. 16*)
- Elizabeth: Hope in the Lord (*Luke 1*)
- Esther: Beauty contest winner (*Esther*)
- Miriam: Courageous older sister (*Num. 12*)
- Ruth: Loyal (*Ruth*)
- Hannah: Full of faith (*1 Sam. 2*)

- Mary and Martha: Sisters - one sat at Jesus' feet while one served (*Joh. 11-12*)
- Huldah: Keeper of the Temple Wardrobe (*2 Chr. 34:14-33*)
- Lydia: Woman of faith who followed Jesus (*Acts 16*)
- Rebekah: Kind, hard worker, and diligent (*Gen. 24-25*)

3. A Good Marriage Is Comprised of Two Good Forgivers

- ❖ Here are wise sayings about forgiveness:
  - May we remember: To forgive is a heroic choice, and it is not for the weak but the strong. (*1 Joh. 4:4*)
  - May we remember: Daily to forgive one another. (*Eph. 4:29-32*)
  - May we remember: Being offended is inevitable, but staying offended is a choice. (*Jam. 3:2; 1 Joh. 2:1*)
  - May we remember: If I go to bed angry with my spouse, I will wake up a little less in love with him/her. (*Eph. 4:26,27*)
  - May we remember: To be a good spouse and parent, one needs to be a good forgiver.
  - May we remember: Couples who struggle to forgive each other are common, but God freely forgave us in Jesus so that we could freely forgive each other.
  - Forgive and you shall be forgiven. (*Luk. 6:37*)
  - Love keeps no record of wrongs. (*1 Cor. 13:5*)
  - Love your neighbor as yourself. (*Lev. 19:18*)

4. Parenting Your Heritage from God

A. Does the following description describe you?
- We are the family provider, servant, and protector. God watches us when we watch over our wives and children. We pray for them and we put them first in everything: our time, our resources, and our patience. We make them laugh. We hold them when they cry. We control our anger. We are generous with our money. We are unselfish. We run from temptations of all kinds. We are loyal. We teach that love is a decision, not a feeling. We keep a promise. We are not critical. We do not hold grudges. We are merciful. We can have joy through the tears. We try not to be irritable or touchy. We are teachable. We do all this and only can do this through the Person and Power of the Holy Spirit.

B. Are You a Patient, Nurturing Father?
- Are you a man who is able to control his emotions, whose emotions do not control him.
- *Proverbs* says, *"He who is slow to anger is better than the mighty"* (*16:32*). A patient man is aware of the connection between an angry heart and offensive speech. He knows that the Holy Spirit wants to control his lips as well as his heart.
- Jesus told us what fuels harsh remarks and arguments: *"For out of the abundance of the heart the mouth speaks"* (*Mat. 12:34*).

C. Encourage wife and children to not be surprised by suffering.
- *Romans 8:18, "For I consider that the sufferings of this present time are not worthy to be compared with the glory which shall be revealed in us."*
- A twentieth-century martyr named Jim Elliot said, "He is no fool who gives what he cannot keep to gain what he cannot lose."
  ▶ Jim harnessed his emotions and responded courageously to God's call to reach the Auca Indians in Ecuador with the Good News of Jesus. He and his teammates were martyred, but their deaths inspired many others to give their lives to God in missions and other noble purposes.
  ▶ Jim and his fellow missionaries were murdered in the 1950's, yet more than five decades later, their honorable life sacrifices continue to inspire people to obey God. Look at how Paul saw such dangerous assignments:
- *"And see, now I go bound in the spirit to Jerusalem, not knowing the things that will happen to me there, except that the Holy Spirit testifies in every city, saying that chains and tribulations await me. But none of these things move me; nor do I count my life dear to myself, so that I may finish my race with joy, and the ministry which I received from the Lord Jesus, to testify to the gospel of the grace of God." (Acts 20:22–24)*

5. Virtues to Pray for Your Kids

❖ Encourage everyone in your church to begin praying these for the young people of your church.
- <u>Salvation</u>: "Lord, let salvation spring up within my children, that they may obtain the salvation that is in Christ Jesus, with eternal glory." *(Isa. 45:8, 2 Tim. 2:10)*
- <u>Growth in Grace</u>: "I pray that my children may grow in the grace and knowledge of our Lord and Savior Jesus Christ." *(2 Pet. 3:18)*
- <u>Love</u>: "Grant, Lord, that my children may learn to live a life of love, through the Spirit who dwells in them." *(Gal. 5:25, Eph. 5:2)*
- <u>Honesty and Integrity</u>: "May integrity and honesty be their virtue and their protection." *(Psa. 25:21)*
- <u>Self-control</u>: "Father, help my children not to be like many others around them, but let them be alert and self-controlled in all they do." *(1 The. 5:6)*
- <u>Love for God's Word</u>: "May my children grow to find Your Word more precious than much pure gold and sweeter than honey from the comb." *(Psa. 19:10)*
- <u>Justice</u>: "God, help my children to love justice as You do and act justly in all they do." *(Psa. 11:7, Mic. 6:8)*
- <u>Mercy</u>: "May my children always be merciful, just as their Father is merciful." *(Luk. 6:36)*
- <u>Respect (for self, others, authority)</u>: "Father, grant that my children may show proper respect to everyone, as your Word commands." *(1 Pet. 2:17)*
- <u>Biblical Self-Esteem</u>: "Help my children develop a strong self-esteem that is rooted in the realization that they are God's workmanship, created in Christ Jesus." *(Eph. 2:10)*
- <u>Faithfulness</u>: "Let love and faithfulness never leave my children, but bind these twin virtues around their necks and write them on the tablet of their hearts." *(Pro. 3:3)*

- Courage: "May my children always be strong and courageous in their character and in their actions." (*Deu. 31:6*)
- Purity: "Create in them a pure heart, O God, and let that purity of heart be shown in their actions." (*Psa. 51:10*)
- Kindness: "Lord, may my children always try to be kind to each other and to everyone else." (*1 The. 5:15*)
- Generosity: "Grant that my children may be generous and willing to share, and so lay up treasure for themselves as a firm foundation for the coming age." (*1 Tim. 6:18-19*)
- Peace-loving: "Father, let my children make every effort to do what leads to peace." (*Rom. 14:19*)
- Joy: "May my children be filled with the joy given by the Holy Spirit." (*1 The. 1:6*)
- Perseverance: "Lord, teach my children perseverance in all they do and help them especially to run with perseverance the race marked out for them." (*Heb. 12:1*)
- Humility: "God, please cultivate in my children the ability to show true humility toward all." (*Titus 3:2*)
- Compassion: "Lord, please clothe my children with the virtue of compassion." (*Col. 3:12*)
- Responsibility: "Grant that my children may learn responsibility, for each one should carry his own load." (*Gal. 6:5*)
- Contentment: "Father, teach my children the secret of being content in any and every situation, through Him who gives them strength." (*Phi. 4:12-13*)
- Faith: "I pray that faith will find root and grow in my children's hearts, that by faith they may gain what has been promised to them." (*Luk. 17:5-6, Heb. 11:1-40*)
- A Servant's Heart: "God, please help my children develop a servants' heart, that by faith they may serve wholeheartedly, as if they were serving the Lord, not men." (*Eph. 6:7*)
- Hope: "May the God of hope grant that my children may overflow with hope and hopefulness by the power of the Holy Spirit." (*Rom. 15:13*)
- Willingness and Ability to Work: "Teach my children, Lord, to value work and to work at it with all their heart, as working for the Lord, not for men." (*Col. 3:23*)
- Passion for God: "Lord, please instill in my children a soul that 'followeth hard after thee', one that clings passionately to you." (*Psa. 63:8*)
- Self-discipline: "Father, I pray that my children may acquire a disciplined and prudent life, doing what is right and just and fair." (*Pro. 1:3*)
- Prayerfulness: "Grant, Lord, that my children's lives may be marked by prayerfulness, that they may learn to pray in the Spirit on all occasions with all kinds of prayers and requests." (*Eph. 6:18*)
- Gratitude: "Help my children to live lives that are always overflowing with thankfulness and always giving thanks to God, the Father, for everything, in the name of our Lord Jesus Christ." (*Eph. 5:20, Col. 2:7*)
- A Heart of Missions: "Lord please help my children to develop a desire to see Your glory declared among the nations, Your marvelous deeds among all peoples." (*Psa. 96:3*)

Endnotes

1. Mark Bailey, Tom Constable, *Nelson's New Testament Survey*, 458.
2. See Dr, Greg Kappas, *Recapturing the Art of Shepherding*, GGN Publications, 2010.
3. A. Duane Liftin, "1 Timothy" in *The Bible Knowledge Commentary*, New Testament Edition, 731.
4. Ibid., 731.
5. Ibid., 731.
6. Ibid., 732.
7. See *Recapturing the Art of Shepherding*.
8. A.T. Robertson, *Word Pictures in the New Testament*, Volume 6.
9. Liftin, "1 Timothy," 732.
10. See *Recapturing the Art of Shepherding*.
11. Charles R. Swindoll, *Excellence in Ministry*, 21.
12. See *Recapturing the Art of Shepherding*.
13. See *Recapturing the Art of Shepherding*.
14. Swindoll, *Excellence in Ministry*, 42.
15. See *Recapturing the Art of Shepherding*.
16. Liftin, "1 Timothy," 738.
17. See *Recapturing the Art of Shepherding*.
18. See *Recapturing the Art of Shepherding*.
19. A. T. Robertson, *Word Pictures in the New Testament*, 4.588.
20. Liftin, "1 Timothy," 744.
21. See *Recapturing the Art of Shepherding*.
22. Swindoll, *Excellence in Ministry*, 103.
23. See *Recapturing the Art of Shepherding*.
24. A. Duane Liftin, "2 Timothy" in *The Bible Knowledge Commentary*, p. 750.
25. Liftin, "2 Timothy," 751.
26. Ibid., 751.
27. See *Recapturing the Art of Shepherding*.
28. Mark Bailey, Tom Constable, *Nelson's New Testament Survey*, 481.
29. Liftin, "2 Timothy," 754.
30. Ibid., 754.
31. Earl Radmacher et al. *Nelson's New Illustrated Bible Commentary*.
32. Liftin, "2 Timothy," 755.
33. See *Recapturing the Art of Shepherding*.
34. See *Recapturing the Art of Shepherding*.
35. Earl Radmacher et al., *Nelson's New Illustrated Bible Commentary*, p. 1617.
36. Ibid., p. 1618.
37. See *Recapturing the Art of Shepherding*.
38. Liftin, "Titus," 762-763.
39. See *Recapturing the Art of Shepherding*.
40. See *Recapturing the Art of Shepherding*.
41. See *Recapturing the Art of Shepherding*.
42. See *Recapturing the Art of Shepherding*.
43. J. Oswald Sanders, *Spiritual Leadership*.
44. J. Oswald Sanders, *Spiritual Leadership*.
45. J. Oswald Sanders, *Spiritual Leadership*.
46. J. Oswald Sanders, *Spiritual Leadership*.
47. See *Recapturing the Art of Shepherding*.

Made in the USA
Columbia, SC
26 May 2018